MW01614711

## Important copyright & legal information

This recipe book is the work of Energise Wat
auction or distribute this workbook. You are NOT a.....
this workbook or its content in any form.

Books, electronic books, or 'ebooks', such as this, are protected under international copyright and intellectual property law. Copyright infringement and theft of intellectual property are serious crimes.

## Medical Disclaimer:

It is essential to remember that none of the Energise Water Ltd employees or directors are:
- a doctor
- a dietitian
- a medical professional
- a journalist
- a therapist

Only opinions based upon our own personal experiences or information detailed in medical/ academic journals or other publications is cited. WE DO NOT OFFER MEDICAL ADVICE or prescribe any treatments. This refers to any form of conversation between Energise UK and our customers, readers or website visitors.

For any health or medical issues consult with your trained health practitioner or Doctor. The recipes and information contained within this book are not a prescription and do not claim to make any health improvements or, in fact, any difference to your health in its own right. Health is a complicated jigsaw of many parts, of which food is only one.

## Notice:

The information contained within this document is for informational and educational purposes only. It is not an attempt by the writers or publisher to diagnose or prescribe, nor should it be construed to be such. Readers are which has been received from sources deemed reliable, but no guarantees, expressed or implied, can be made regarding the accuracy of same. Therefore, readers are also encouraged to verify for themselves and to their own satisfaction the accuracy of all reports, recommendations, conclusions, comments, opinions, or anything else published herein before making any kind of decisions based upon what they have read. If you have a medical condition, please consult your medical practitioner.

**For full terms and conditions visit: http://www.alkalinewatermadeeasy.com/policies**

# Praise for The Alkaline Diet Recipe Book

"I LOVE THIS BOOK! The fresh, easy, delicious receipes and beautiful photos make it a joy to use and an inspiration to anyone wanting to improve their health and vitality with the alkaline diet.

Really inspiring and exactly what's needed!

I'm sure it will inspire many people and I'm so pleased to have my copy!"

**Rose Elliot, MBE**
*Best-Selling Author of 3.5 million cookb•
and Briatin's favourite vegetarian chef.*

"The Alkaline Diet Recipe Book is an inspiring "how to" manual for fun and tasty, genuinely healthy eating. This book is packed with tasty, nutritious and inspiring menu plans that are quick and easy to make. Ross's enthusiasm for the subject shines through in every page. If you're serious about your health, download or buy it ..... now!

I'll definitely be recommending this book to my patients. It should make my job as a pH, food focused nutritional therapist a lot easier!"

**Gareth Edwards, BSc. DiplON. mBAN**
*www.food-for-life.co.uk*

"Even my husband Is loving It! I absolutely love this recipe book. I have looked forward to cooking something different from it every day. Recipes are so easy and extremely tasty.

Its lovely blending all the fresh Ingredients, making delicious meals and not spending hours in the kitchen. My husband who loves meat is really enjoying it too! Thank you so much. "

**Review by Ash, U**

"Answer to a Prayer! At last, a reasonably priced , fully comprehensive collection of recipes to make alkalizing a simple, easy, yet delicious experience.

It's great to know that whichever tasty one I choose will not only give my body the food It needs, but it wont require rare and costly ingredients!"

**Review by Pearl, USA**

"I've tried to get alkaline before, but I've always fallen off the wagon. This has been IDEAL for me!

I've lost 7kg so far and feel great! And a lot less tired! I also have less mood swings and I'm clearer mentally and much more confident!"

**Review by Nikki, Australi•**

# Contents

# Who is Ross Bridgeford?

Ross Bridgeford is a writer, health coach and nutrition addict & his dream is to ENERGIZE the World.

His dream started in 2004 with the creation of energiseforlife.com, where he has published over 00 guides, recipes and articles, read by over 2 million people every year.

Ross is the author of two Alkaline Diet Recipe Books (including this one!) and the Amazon best-seller "The Water Diet".

Ross has also coached thousands of clients to their dream health through his courses: The Alkaline Diet Course, The Alkaline Weight Loss Solution & the Alkaline Cleanse Programme.

## My Mission...

I am driven to help you nourish your body, unleash the energy within you and to give you everything you need to live with the vitality, passion and body of your dreams.

I am driven to give you everything you need to have the energy to live your best life.

This is my call to arms. I want you to join me.

When we live with energy, every other area of our life improves.

When we nourish our body and live with energy, we live with positivity.

It effects every area of our lives: our relationships, our finances, our ability to push ourselves and take on new goals and challenges, our ability to grow, our career...all of this is positively impacted by having energy.

In fact, living a fulfilled life without energy and without a healthy body is practically impossible.

Getting rid of excess weight, symptoms like IBS, reflux, gout, arthritis, candida, eczema, chronic fatigue...relief from these things will all come from nourishing the body.

It will happen.

And once they're taken care of you will have a body that is thriving and energised.

# Having ENERGY Can Change the World

Living energized has a ripple effect.

When we live with energy and nourish ourselves it has a knock on effect to those around us.

Our relationship with our partner and our kids is lifted, our outlook on life and the way we react to life challenges is different. The way we interact at work is positive…we make those around us react differently.

The people around us start to make more positive decisions, they smile more, they influence others in more optimistic and productive way.

## Together we can create a movement & a force for change in the World...

My belief is that if I can educate and motivate one person to nourish their body to live with energy and they can impact one person, I am a happy man.

If I can influence 10 people who can then influence 20 then together we can create a movement. And want you to join me in this movement for change & positivity in the world.

Let's live with energy, nourish ourselves and create our best life ever."

*Ross Bridgeford*

# What is The Alkaline Diet?

The alkaline diet is a very, very simple and straightforward approach to health, but is backed by extensive science.

**Now, before I explain just how simple it is, here is the explanation in scientific terms:**

Our body is designed to be alkaline.

The pH of our important fluids such as our blood is designed to be at a pH of 7.365, which is slightly alkaline. In just the same way that our body will do whatever it takes to regulate our temperature to stay within a very tight range, it does the same for the pH of our fluids.

And while our body does create acids naturally through our bodily functions, we have a small alkaline buffering system that works to neutralise these acids created by our body through it's day to day activities.

Your body HAS to keep the pH of your blood, cells and other fluids at this slightly alkaline level (pH 7.365) and it will do ANYTHING it has to in order to maintain this pH balance.

To do this, your body calls upon this store of alkaline buffers, which is perfectly adequate when we are living a natural, healthy diet.

However, this store of buffers is very easily depleted because most of us eat and drink such strong acidic foods and do very little exercise - while our lifestyles of high stress, smoking, drinking and getting too little sleep only compounds this problem.

To put this in context, the pH scale is logarithmic – so pH 6 is 10x more acidic than pH 7, pH 5 is 100x times more acidic than pH 7 and pH 4 is 1000x more acidic.

Cola has a pH of between 2 and 3.

So you can see how a diet filled with meats, dairy, fizzy drinks, alcohol etc would quickly deplete these buffers as it would take a solution that is somewhere between 10000 and 100000 times more alkaline than cola to balance this out.

And when we deplete these buffers and still ingest more acids…what happens?

The body is forced into drawing upon the alkaline minerals it has to buffer which causes havoc in the body – for instance, if the body is constantly drawing calcium to neutralise the acids we consume then the symptoms of osteoporosis emerge (hence the recent scientific studies linking cola consumption with osteoporosis).

As we have evolved over the last century our diets and lifestyles have dramatically increased the amount of acidity in our lives. Diet, stress, emotions and no exercise all contribute to the increased acidity in our body.

I'm sure it will be of no surprise to you to learn that the most acidic foods are sugar, trans-fats, yeasts, dairy, simple carbs, alcohol, refined foods etc. These acids manifest in our diets as colas & fizzy drinks, pizza, chips, cakes, biscuits, microwave meals, crisps, breads, caffeine, cheese, take-aways, fatty meats, ice cream, smoking, beers, wines, condiments, milky drinks, cream etc. all the foods you already know are not good for you.

I'm sure you can guess that the foods that are alkaline to the body are therefore...wait for it...fresh vegetables, salads, leafy greens, omega oils, nuts, seeds, pulses, whole grains. These are fresh foods, whole foods and foods with a high-water content and nutritional value.

It makes this diet pretty easy to understand and pretty easy to follow. I think most people, if given a list of foods could put them into the acid or alkaline group 8 times out of 10.

# So, what makes a food acid or alkaline?

There are a couple of scientific variables, but to keep it simple, these are the most important rules to help guide your food choices:

1.    If a food is high in alkaline minerals including magnesium, potassium, calcium or sodium it is likely to be alkaline to the body.

2.    BUT - regardless of its alkaline mineral content, if it contains any of the following then it will be acidifying:

> O    SUGAR
> O    YEAST
> O    IS FERMENTED (LIKE SOY SAUCE)
> O    CONTAINS FUNGI (LIKE MUSHROOMS)
> O    IS REFINED/MICROWAVED/PROCESSED

One confusing food for most people who transition to an alkaline diet is fruit - which, unfortunately is acid-forming, due to its high sugar content. I know that fruit contains a lot of good stuff too, such as fibre, vitamins and minerals - however, this high sugar content really does undo anything the good stuff can bring.

Bananas for example are very high in potassium, but are around 25% sugar. The only exceptions to the 'no fruit rule' are tomatoes, avocados, lemons & limes (great for dressings and flavourings), grapefruit and watermelon (to some degree) which are alkaline because they are so low in sugar.

# The Problem With Sugar

Sugar is such an issue because when it is consumed it immediately and dramatically affects the pH of the blood and causes massive damage to the body.

As explained above, when the blood deviates from pH 7.365 it causes major stress to the rest of the body. The body has to maintain this pH level and it will go to quite extreme measures to make sure it stays there.

Why?

Because in an acidic state, red blood cells cannot function as they are supposed to and in this state they begin a biological transformation into bacteria and yeast (this transformation is called pleomorphism) and pollute your internal environment.

In addition, the acids that are created and consumed in our modern lifestyle also ferment in the blood, and create harmful by-products, toxins and alcohols, which then further destroy our internal environment.

In short, the lengths the body has to (and will) go to in order to maintain this alkaline pH causes damage to almost every other area of the body, and the knock on effects of an over-acid system compound this even more and a vicious cycle begins that leaves you sick and tired.

Consuming sugar is like throwing petrol on a fire.

Sugar immediately ferments and causes absolute havoc in the body. And with more acid and sugar, more toxins are created, the pH is lowered, the bacteria and yeast grows, becomes mold, and a vicious cycle begins.

The unfriendly toxins, yeasts, bacteria and mold created by this sugar consumption and acidic environment not only cause your system to become polluted and stressed, but they also feed off your good nutrients (meaning you feel less of the benefit of the good things you do eat) and excrete toxic acid waste, making the blood even more acidic and polluted.

This toxic waste is…acid.

It also acts as a food to the yeasts and bacteria already there, further fuelling the problem.

So:

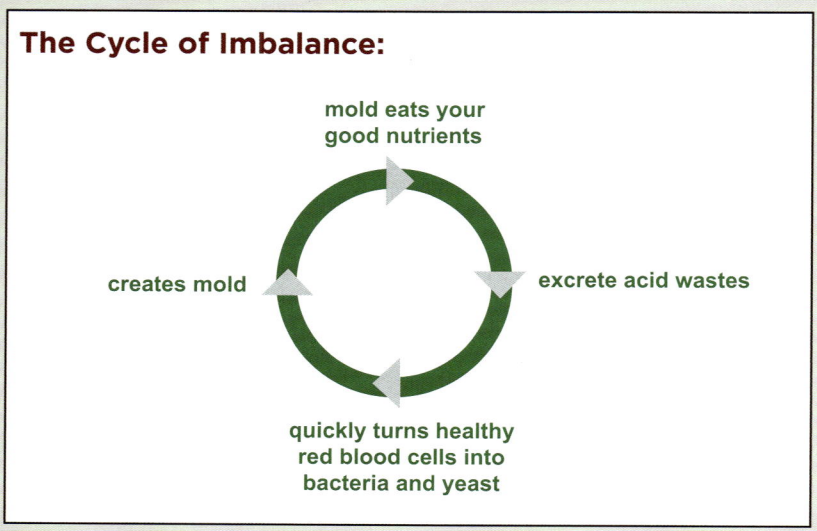

**The Cycle of Imbalance:**

mold eats your good nutrients

excrete acid wastes

quickly turns healthy red blood cells into bacteria and yeast

creates mold

Emotions, stress and a lack of exercise all contribute to this. In fact, emotions can have twice as much of an effect on our blood and health as any food can. Exercise is obviously essential becaus it pumps our blood and lymph around the body to remove wastes and helps to deliver oxygen to cells for necessary functioning.

So there you have it - that is the scientific, long version.

# Here is the simple version:

Our body is designed to stay alkaline and will do whatever it takes to do so. When we consume acidic foods and drinks, stop exercising and continually have negative emotions our body is overru with acids and this causes major disruption.

Not surprisingly the acid foods are the ones you already know are bad for you (cola, chips, chocolate, sweets, burgers, dairy, beer etc) and the alkaline foods are the ones you already know are good for you (fresh foods, leafy green vegetables, salads, nuts, seeds etc).

To become alkaline you simply need to start focusing 70-80% of your diet on the alkaline foods and try to limit the acid foods. Back this up with 3-4 litres of good quality, clean, filtered water each day and you will be very pleasantly surprised by the way you feel.

**So follow your mother's advice and eat your greens!**

For more explanation and scientific evidence, citations and research visit us at liveenergized.com o contact ross@liveenergized.com

# My Philosophy on Health
### And The Answer To The Question 'Do I Have To Give Up Everything?'

### Why Live Energized is Different

Recently, as part of my Alkaline Cleanse Coaching Course, I was forced to sit and think about my philosophy towards treats, snacking, naughty foods, nights out and willpower, and then try express how I've made the alkaline diet work for me.

The thought of giving up some of your favourite foods, drinks and social eating and drinking is really scary for us when we first commit to living alkaline - so I hope my philosophy puts you at ease!

## Treating Treats as Treats

So...a question I often get asked is:

> Ross...Will I have to give up EVERYTHING...FOREVER?!

And my honest answer is,

> No, of course not.

I think this is where I differ from most health, diet and alkaline diet folks and I think this is another reason why I get such a high success rate with my customers and clients in my training programmes.

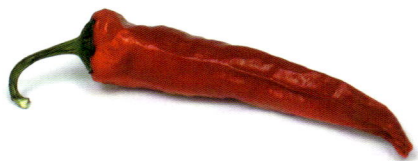

# Here is my philosophy:

I believe that success with this lifestlye is guaranteed when you don't change who you are at your core. You should still be social, you should still have treats, you should still be naughty, you should still enjoy life!

I guarantee that you are FAR more likely to succeed if you are 80% great and 20% relaxed than if you try to be 100% perfect.  Still go out for dinner.  Still have a glass of wine.  Still enjoy your occassional espresso.  Just don't go overboard or out of control.

Life is about enjoyment and moderation in both directions is essential. Don't feel that you're giving up your life.

When you come from this perspective you will find that the more you become healthy, vibrant and alkaline the more you will ACTUALLY want to treat these foods and drinks as treats because you PREFER the feeling of living healthy.

What a great place to be!

I would never say you HAVE to do anything, listen to your body and remember: stress, guilt, deprivation, and all other negative emotions can be twice as acidifying to the blood than diet.

Now this isn't me giving you the green light to be as bad with everything as you are good. There are still things that I would definitely aim to transition away from as soon as possible such as tobacco, colas/sodas, saturated fats and deep fried foods, but you can certainly pick your treats so that you really enjoy them when you have them.

For instance, I never, ever drink fizzy drinks or eat sweets. Ever. But if I go out to dinner I'll be pretty relaxed with what I order. I'll probably still get a great big green salad on the side, but I won't be too shy with what I eat. And at the time I love it and feel really rewarded, and the next day I wake up and just get back on and have a nice vegetable juice and I'm away...

Try to take this philosophy forward with you. Treat treats as a treat, and just make the right decisions 80% of the time.   I promise you that you will be a lot happier and more likely to succeed with your diet.

# How To Use This Book

While this is, of course, just a recipe book - it is a very important recipe book that actually does more than just give you some recipes!

**NOT KNOWING WHAT TO COOK IS THE #1 REASON WHY MOST PEOPLE STRUGGLE WITH THE ALKALINE DIET**

This book provides the fundamental basis on which you can build your alkaline lifestyle. As I explained above, my number one goal for this book was to give you real food - real recipes - that you could actually cook and enjoy.

So as you go through this book and start to incorporate these recipes into your life I recommend you do so with the following three principles in mind:

**1** **Go Slow**: I've been helping people to successfully transition to an alkaline lifestyle for many years now and the most obvious difference to me between those who succeed and those who fail is that those who succeed - 99% of the time - go slow and take it easy. They transition. When people go cold turkey (no pun intended) they usually only last a few days, if that.

**2** **Find Your Faves**: Something that really helped me to make this lifestyle permanent was working out the meals that a) I enjoyed the most; b) found quickest and easiest to cook; and c) frequently had the right ingredients for. Go through the book and pick four or five of these and make sure you've always got the core ingredients of that meal in the pantry.

**3** **Plan Ahead**: Being underprepared is the next biggest reason why people fail to reach their health goals. When the fridge is empty - we snack. And when the fridge is empty, the snacks are always unhealthy. The same goes for takea- way - it is almost always ordered when we don't have any- thing in to cook! So go through this recipe book, pick out your meals for the week and then shop for them a few days in advance!

13

# A Few Notes...

## Translations!

I am UK-based and therefore I'm always writing in UK-English. Sorry about that. As a few of you reading this might be based elsewhere I thought it might be handy to include a few conversions and translations.

| UK | Non-UK |
|---|---|
| Aubergine | Eggplant |
| Courgette | Zucchini |
| Coriander | Cilantro |
| Beetroot | Beets |
| Broad Beans | Fava Beans |
| Chard | Silver Beet |
| Chickpeas | Garbanzo Beans |
| Haricot Beans | Navy Beans |
| Mangetout | Snowpeas |
| Pepper | Capsicum or Sweet Pepper |
| Rocket | Arugula |
| Spring Onions | Scallions |
| Stock | Broth |
| Stock Cube | Bouillon Cubes |

## Cooking Conversions

1 militers = 1/5 teaspoon
5 ml = 1 teaspoon
15 ml = 1 tablespoon
34 ml = 1 fluid oz.
100 ml = 3.4 fluid oz.
240 ml = 1 cup
1 liter = 34 fluid oz.
1 liter = 4.2 cups
1 liter = 2.1 pints
1 liter = 1.06 quarts
1 liter = .26 gallon

16 tablesppns = 1 cup
12 tablespoons = 3/4 cup
10 tablespoons + 2 teaspoons = 2/3 cup
8 tablespoons = 1/2 cup
6 tablespoons = 3/8 cup
5 tablespoons + 1 teaspoon = 1/3 cup
4 tablespoons = 1/4 cup
2 tablespoons = 1/8 cup
2 tablespoons + 2 teaspoons = 1/6 cup
1 tablespoon = 1/16 cup
2 cups = 1 pint
2 pints = 1 quart
3 teaspoons = 1 tablespoon
48 teaspoons = 1 cup

1 gram = .035 ounce
100 grams = 3.5 ounces
500 grams = 1.10 pounds
1 kilogram = 2.205 pounds
1 kilogram = 35 oz.

# Juices & Smoothies

Juices and smoothies are about to become your friend. Packed full of goodness, these alkaline superstars are quick, easy, satisfying, filling and are an incredibly dense source of nutrients.

How else could you fit a whole cucumber, two sticks of celery, handfuls of spinach, kale, lettuce, bell pepper and more into one single serve. You can get all of that nutrition into one drink! Imagine having your five daily serves of vegetables knocked off  before you've left the house!

Enjoy at breakfast, lunch or as a snack during the day!

# Live Energized Alkaline Green Drink

The core green-drink and my most popular recipe!

**Serves:** 2
**Preparation Time:** 10 Minutes

**Ingredients:**
2 sticks of celery
1 cucumber (medium to large)
2 large handfuls of spinach leaves
1 large handful of lettuce (any-
dark green preferably)

**Optional:**
Lemon/Lime - freshly squeezed
Green powder
pH drops
Kale
Parsley
Any other greens (just nothing
onion or garlic-based!)

**Instructions:**

**1** Thoroughly wash all of the ingredients and slice thinly enough to pass through the juicer. I recommend that you cut the celery into quite small pieces as the stringy fibres can get caught up in the juicer, especially if you are using a masticating juicer.

**2** Once all of the ingredients have been juiced, add the green powder and pH drops and stir thoroughly. If you find the taste too 'vegetable-y' you can squeeze in fresh lemon or lime. This makes it both more alkaline and tasty!

**Note:** This is a highly alkaline green drink. I personally drink this more than any other juice or smoothie. It is fresh, nutritious and keeps me buzzing for hours!

# Ultimate Alkaline Liver Cleanse Juice

The Easiest, most cleansing juice for the liver - and it is just so refreshing.

**Serves:** 2
**Preparation Time:** 5 Minutes

**Ingredients:**
2 large grapefruits
4 lemons
300ml of water (preferably filtered
2 tablespoons of Udo's Choice (
cold pressed flax oil)
1-2 cloves of fresh garlic
2 inches of fresh root ginger

**Optional:**
A dash of cayenne pepper!

**Instructions:**

**1** Squeeze the juice of the grapefruit and lemon into a blender by hand.

**2** Next, grate the garlic and the ginger, and then using a garlic press, squeeze this into the juice.

**3** Now add the water, Udo's Choice and blend for 30 seconds.

**4** Add more ginger/garlic to taste and enjoy cold!

# Alkaline Avocado Power Shake!

Filling, nutritious, alkaline and satisfying - keeps you on top of your game for hours!

**Serves:** 2
**Preparation Time:** 15 Minutes

**Ingredients:**
1 cucumber
2 tomatoes
1 avocado
1 handful spinach leaves
1 lime
½ red pepper
½ teaspoon vegetable stock
1 scoop Mega Greens (optional)
1 scoop Super Soy Sprouts (optional)
1 tablespoon Udo's Choice (optional)

**Instructions:**

**1** Wash all of the ingredients thoroughly and then chop the cucumber, tomato, pepper and avocado roughly.

**2** Dissolve the vegetable stock in a small amount (50ml) of warm water.

**3** Place the avocado and stock in the blender and mix into a paste.

**4** Next, add the high water content ingredients (cucumber, tomato etc) into a blender and blend until they are becoming more liquid.

**5** Finally add the spinach, lime and supplements and blend until all ingredients are thoroughly mixed.

Serve in a tall glass.

# Blood Builder Vegetable Juice

Containing plenty of nature's blood builder - chlorophyll - this juice will have you alkaline in no time!

**Serves:** 2
**Preparation Time:** 10 Minutes

**Ingredients:**
1 cucumber
2 large handfuls spinach
Handful parsley
1 stick celery
Handful of kale

**Optional:**
You can also add 15 drops
of Dr Young's ChloropHeal to
really boost the blood building
goodness of this juice!

**Instructions:**

**1** Wash all ingredients thoroughly, slice and juice in a (preferably)
masticating juicer.

If you only have a centrifugal juicer for now, this is fine. The
difference between the two is that the masticating juicer retains
more nutrients.

# Ginger Zinger

This tea is perfect for a hot or cold day and is a cleansing pick-me-up!

**Serves:** 2
**Preparation Time:** 10 Minutes

**Ingredients:**
500ml alkaline water
2 inch ginger finger
2 lemons

**Instructions:**

**1** Grate the ginger, keeping the 'pulp' and put it all into a blender alongside the water and the juice of the two lemons.

**2** Blend for 30 seconds and serve.

**Note:** Used warmed water in winter, or add a finely sliced red chilli for extra zing.

# Almond Maca Smoothie

A libido-boosting smoothie that is smooth, sexy and satisfying!

**Serves:** 2
**Preparation Time:** 10 Minutes

**Ingredients:**
1 banana
350ml soy or almond milk (p33)
2 tablespoons almond butter
1 teaspoon maca powder
Dash of vanilla or almond extract

**Instructions:**

**1** Chop the banana and blend all ingredients to form a smoothie! Easy!

**Note:** This is not the most alkaline recipe (due to the banana) so use sparingly as a treat or if on a libido boosting diet!

# pH Boosting Protein Shake

An alkaline smoothie with that extra protein kick to build muscle after a workout!

**Serves:** 2
**Preparation Time:** 15 Minutes

**Ingredients:**
1 avocado
1 lime
1 cucumber (add more or less to change consistency)
Silken tofu 1/2 to 1 slab/packet
Soy milk or almond milk (add to get the consistency you want)
1-2 big handfuls of fresh raw spinach leaves
Ice to taste (if your blender can handle ice)

**Instructions:**

**1** Peel the avocado and lime and thoroughly wash the cucumber (if it is a thick skinned cucumber, peel some of this away).

**2** Then place all of the ingredients into a blender and whizz it all up. If you are particularly keen on lime then you can garnish with some of the zest!

**Note:** This recipe, in my opinion works best with limes, but if you are keen on lemons that try that too (or a combination of both!)

Dependent upon how much tofu and soy milk you use, this can pack a punch of about 20g of protein per drink - which is not far off most of the vegan-unfriendly, acid-forming, whey-based protein shakes and powders.

# Garlic & Ginger Tonic Tea

Cleansing anti-fungal, anti-toxin, anti-acid tea! Better for you than coffee, eh?

**Serves:** 2-4
**Preparation Time: 20** Minutes

**Ingredients:**
4 cloves of garlic, minced
4 chunks of root ginger, grated
1 lemon, juiced
A small dash of cayenne pepper

**Instructions:**

**1** Prepare all ingredients as above and place in a large pot.

**2** Boil enough alkaline water to serve the desired number of people the desired amount!

**3** Once boiled, let it rest for a minute and then cover the ingredients and infuse for 15 minutes.

Strain and drink. Or for extra goodness, don't strain!

# Sexy Smoothie

This smoothie will ignite your sex-drive like nothing else! Beware - it really does work!

**Serves:** 2
**Preparation Time:** 15 Minutes

**Ingredients:**
2 sticks of celery
3 asparagus stalks
1/2 avocado
1/2 cucumber
Handful spinach
Pumpkin seeds
1 clove of garlic
Linseed, Sunflower & Almond
(LSA) meal

**Instructions:**

**1**   Roughly chop all of the ingredients.

**2**   Juice the celery & asparagus and then put in a blender with the
remaining ingredients. Add lemon or lime juice if desired.

**Note:** garlic is, believe it or not, great for the libido - but note,
if you're hoping for an immediate effect then maybe leave the
garlic out - it is raw, and it may taint the desirability of your
mouth for a short while!

# Sweet Green Drink

A transitional green drink incorporating the sweeter veggies

**Serves:** 2
**Preparation Time: 10** Minutes

**Ingredients:**
3 carrots
1 cucumber
1 green pepper
1 beetroot (medium)
2 tomatoes
1 inch of ginger

**Instructions:**

**1**  Thoroughly wash all ingredients and chop them roughly.

**2**  Juice everything but hold some cucumber back to juice after the ginger to wash all of this through the juicer. There is no need to peel the ginger if you wash it thoroughly or buy organic.

**Note:** This is a relatively high-sugar juice so you should only have this as a treat or when transitioning. If you find the taste of the Energise Green Drink too vegetable-y then you can use this drink as a transition as you get used to the subtle sweetness of vegetables.

# Skin Clear Juice

A great juice to help with problem skin, or to just make your skin more soft, supple and beautiful!

**Serves:** 2
**Preparation Time: 10** Minutes

**Ingredients:**
2 medium potatoes
2 sticks of celery
1 cucumber
2 carrots
1 handful of spinach or watercress (or both!)

**Instructions:**

**1** Wash and peel the potatoes and carrots (unless organic) and roughly chop all of the ingredients.

**2** Juice everything and enjoy!

**Note:** If you supplement with the greens, pH drops and omega oils (such as Udo's Choice) you will find your skin to be much improved in no time!

# Delicious Refresher Juice

Tried to think of a better name for this one, but thought…nah…why not - it does what it says on the tin!

**Serves:** 2
**Preparation Time: 10** Minutes

**Ingredients:**
2 grapefruits
2 celery stalks
1 carrot
1 inch of fresh ginger
150ml alkaline water (or dilute to taste)

**Instructions:**

**1** Thoroughly wash all of the ingredients and peel the grapefruit and ginger.

**2** Juice everything and enjoy! Serve over ice on a hot day…

# Alkaline Margarita!

One for the summer afternoons!

**Serves:** 2
**Preparation Time: 10** Minutes

**Ingredients:**
1 lemon
2 limes
4 sticks of celery
1 cucumber
1 inch stick of fresh root ginger
Optional: Himalayan salt

**Instructions:**

**1** Peel the lemon and lime and juice through your juicer or just halve and juice by hand. Peel the ginger and juice this next.

**2** Juice everything else and enjoy! Add more ginger if you like it to have a bit more of a spicy, gingery kick! You could even roll the edge with Himalayan salt!

You can water it down to taste if you find it a bit sharp!

# Sweet & Chunky Alkaline Shake

Another simple one, just wash your veggies, blend and enjoy!

**Serves:** 2
**Preparation Time: 10** Minutes

**Ingredients:**
1 cucumber
4 tomatoes
1 avocado
2 sticks of celery
1 red pepper
2 broccoli heads & stalks
A few basil leaves
50ml vegetable stock

**Instructions:**

**1** Wash all of the ingredients thoroughly and then chop the cucumber, tomato, pepper and avocado roughly. Slice the celery thinly to stop the stringy fibres clogging up the blender.

**2** Place the avocado and stock in the blender and whizz into a paste.

**3** Now throw in the remaining ingredients and blend until there is a slightly chunky consistency.

Serve in a tall glass and enjoy!

# Raw Almond Milk

Quick and easy to make and brilliant in smoothies, on muesli or on it's own!

**Serves:** 4
**Preparation Time:** 20 Minutes

**Ingredients:**
1 cup almonds
3 cups water
1 vanilla bean, seeds scooped out

**Instructions:**

**1** Soak the almonds in water overnight in an airtight container in the fridge. Drain the old water and then blend the almonds with the new water (3 cups) until it is pretty much all nice and smooth.

**2** Now strain with a cheesecloth or other strainer and voilà!

It will keep for about 3 days in the fridge. Enjoy with your alkaline muesli!

# Other Breakfasts

While juices and smoothies will make up a large proportion of your breakfasts on an alkaline diet, these tasty metabolism starters are fantastic when you are first starting out, or when you have only got a few minutes before you race out of the door.

Remember, as you become more accustomed to the subtle sweetness of the alkaline vegetables you might find yourself enjoying some of the lunch and dinner meals at breakfast-time too!

# Transition Breakfast Muesli

A great transition breakfast muesli- giving you nutrition and moving you towards alkalinity

**Serves:** 2
**Preparation Time: 5** Minutes

**Ingredients:**
Organic oats
Handful almonds
Handful walnuts
Handful dried cranberries
1 banana
1 spoon natural live bio-yoghurt
Soy or rice milk to taste

**Instructions:**

**1** Mix ingredients together and serve with your milk of choice and the yoghurt on top!

See page 20 for a Raw Almond Milk recipe!

**Note:** this recipe is HIGHLY transitional. As you aim to become more and more alkaline substitute out the yoghurt, banana and cranberries and instead add more alkaline nuts and seeds such as pumpkin seeds, sunflower seeds and if necessary a soy yoghurt.

# Alkaline Fibre Muesli

A high-fibre brekkie to get your digestive system kick-started!

**Serves:** 2
**Preparation Time: 5** Minutes

**Ingredients:**
Toasted oats
Handful almond meal
Small handful psyllium husks
Finely sliced almonds
Finely sliced sunflower seeds
Handful buckwheat
1/2 grated apple
Sprinkle or cinnamon and nutmeg
Soy/rice/almond milk to taste

**Instructions:**

**1** Mix ingredients together to form a muesli and add as much of your chosen milk as you desire.

**Note:** again, this muesli is quite transitional. Substitute the apple out as you become more alkaline.

You can find almond meal & buckwheat in most major supermarkets these days, but if not then health food stores always stock this.

Psyllium husks are available from www.energiseforlife.com

# Omega Muesli

Tasty muesli that is high in omega 3 - which is great for your skin!

**Serves:** 2
**Preparation Time: 5** Minutes

**Ingredients:**
Spelt oats
1/2 cup of LSA mix (linseed, sunflower seed and almond meal)
Handful of thinly sliced almonds
Handful of pumpkin seeds
Soy/almond/rice milk to taste

**Instructions:**

**1** Mix ingredients and add milk of your choice. See page 33 for an alkaline almond milk recipe that is very, very delicious.

# Seedy Breakfast

A crunchy mix of healthy seeds to get you on your way

**Serves:** 2
**Preparation Time: 5** Minutes

**Ingredients:**
2 cups of sunflower seeds
2 cups of pumpkin seed
2 cups of almonds
2 cups of sesame seeds
1 grated apple
Alkaline water
25ml soy milk (or to your chosen consistency)

**Instructions:**

**1**  Soak the seed mix and grated apple in alkaline water and soy milk (just enough to cover the seeds) for three hours.

**2**  When it is ready you can add more soy milk to taste.

# Avocado Breakfast On-the-Go

Highly nutritious brekkie that can be enjoyed at a snack at any time during the day

**Serves:** 2
**Preparation Time: 5** Minutes

**Ingredients:**
1 avocado
1/2 lemon
Small handful sesame seeds
Flax Oil or Udo's Choice
1 clove of garlic
1 tomato or four cherry tomatoes
A pinch of Himalayan salt/sea salt

**Instructions:**

**1** Dice the tomato, crush the garlic and spoon out the avocado, keeping the skin intact.

**2** Mix everything together with the lemon and oil and then place back into empty avocado skin, sprinkle with Himalayan salt, sesame seeds and serve.

# Alkaline Baked Bean Salsa Brekkie

Look at all of those alkalising, energising ingredients! A great start to the day!

**Serves:** 2
**Preparation Time:** 30 Minutes

**Ingredients:**
1 can of haricot beans
4 spring onions
6 cherry tomatoes
1 handful of basil
2 handfuls of spinach
2 cloves of garlic
1 avocado
½ lemon
Olive oil
Himalayan salt & black pepper

**Instructions:**

**1** Roughly chop the spring onions, halve the cherry tomatoes, and finely chop the garlic. Now, in a reasonably sized frying pan, bring a little water to the boil (maybe 50ml or less) and 'steam fry' the garlic for one minute.

**2** Now throw in the cherry tomatoes, haricot beans and spring onions until everything softens. This should only take a minute.

**3** Next add the basil and spinach until it is just wilted and season with Himalayan salt and black pepper.

**4** While this is cooking prepare a side salad and halve the avocado and voilà.

**5** Serve the bean salsa mix with salad and the halved avocado, with lemon and olive oil drizzled all over.

# Scrambled Tofu & Tomato Brekkie

A real treat to give you that big, cooked breakfast feel on a Sunday

**Serves:** 2
**Preparation Time:** 15 Minutes

**Ingredients:**

285g regular firm tofu
1 tablespoon coconut oil
2 tomatoes
½ brown onion
½ small red pepper
Pinch of turmeric
Freshly ground black pepper
Himalayan/Sea salt
A little basil

**Instructions:**

**1** This is really easy, and really quick. Simply dice or crumble the tofu in your hands into a bowl. Now chop and quickly fry off the onion in the coconut oil and dice the pepper and do the same.

**2** Now dice the tomatoes and throw these in with the tofu and a pinch of tumeric. Grind in your pepper and salt and cook until the tofu is warm and ready. Right at the last throw in some torn basil leaves and serve!

**3** I like to serve it on some toasted, sprouted bread and with some baby spinach leaves drizzled with olive oil.

**Note:** coconut oil is the only safe oil to cook with. It has an extremely high resistance to heat, light and oxygen so can withstand cooking. **All** other oils become highly toxic when exposed to heat, light or air.

# Soups

These alkaline soups are a fast, easy, tasty way to get a whole heap of raw veggies into your diet.

Brilliant for snacks, lunch and dinner these filling and satisfying soups can all be enjoyed warm or chilled.

Pretty much all of these soups are 100% alkaline, and many are totally raw (even when warmed) so feel free to make them in large quantities and take to work for a mid-morning or mid-afternoon snack.

# Warming Alkaline Broccoli Soup

A great one for a cold day or when you just need something warming and hearty!

**Serves:** 2
**Preparation Time:** 20 Minutes

**Ingredients:**
1 large broccoli
1 cucumber
1 finger of ginger
1 handful of spinach
1 handful of rocket
1 garlic clove
Juice of 1/2 lemon or lime
1/2 avocado
100ml vegetable stock (yeast & salt free/reduced)

**Instructions:**

**1**    Steam the broccoli for 8-10 minutes.

**2**    Blend the avocado and vegetables stock.

**3**    Next blend the cucumber, spinach, rocket, garlic and ginger (sliced very thin).

**4**    Finally add the warmed broccoli and blend

**5**    This should give nice warmth to the soup, but if you need it warmer, warm gently in a pan (don't cook, you should be able to comfortably put your finger in without burning). Once you've served into bowls, squeeze over the lemon or lime.

# Raw Italian Summer Soup

This was first posted on our blog three years ago - and has had hundreds of glowing reviews since!

**Serves:** 2
**Preparation Time:** 15 Minutes

**Ingredients:**
1 avocado (add more for extra creaminess)
6 tomatoes, skinned
A generous bunch of basil
1/4 of a cup of cold pressed oil (olive, hemp or blend)

**Instructions:**

**1** Place the avocado (peeled and stoned), skinned tomato, basil and oil into a blender and whizz until smooth.

For extra smoothness you can put through a sieve (removes the tomato pips). If you prefer it a little 'thinner' juice a cucumber and add.

**Note:** I also like to have a drizzle of oil on the top and also to rip a few extra basil leaves on top.

Tip: to skin the tomatoes, place them in a big bowl of boiled water for a minute or so, then remove one at a time and pierce the skin - the skin should just slip away!

# Autumn Tomato & Avocado Warmer

A slightly warm soup that is still a little summery!

**Serves:** 2
**Preparation Time:** 20 Minutes

**Ingredients:**
5 large ripe tomatoes
1 ripe avocado
1 spring onion
1/4 cup ground almonds (freshly done yourself, not packet)
1 cup broth from Swiss Vegetable bouillon
1/4 teaspoon dill seed
Dash cayenne pepper
Sea salt & cracked black pepper to taste

**Instructions:**

**1** Place all of the ingredients into a blender (except one of the tomatoes) and blend!

**2** Depending on whether you are going cold or warm - then place the soup into a pan and warm very slightly. Warming so that it is not painful to put your finger into still means that the soup is raw.

**3** Now dice the remaining tomato and sprinkle on top to serve!

# Warming Squash Soup

A very popular soup in my house. It's not raw but it is nutrient dense, filling and smoothing

**Serves:** 2
**Preparation Time:** 40 Minutes

**Ingredients:**
1 large butternut squash
1 brown onion
350ml water
1 spoon of yeast-free vegetable bouillon
1 can of coconut milk
Sprinkle of nutmeg
Himalayan salt and cracked black pepper to taste.

**Instructions:**

**1** Bring the water and stock to the boil.

**2** While this is heating, chop the squash into small chunks, removing the skin and the seeds (keep the seeds for roasting if you like - they're delicious!)

**3** Slice the onion and then add all of the ingredients to the boiling stock.

**4** Lower the heat and simmer until all ingredients are soft and then blend smooth.

Serve with an extra sprinkle of nutmeg and a smile.

# Alkaline Gazpacho

Straight from Madrid - this Spanish speciality is alkaline - nice Juan!

**Serves:** 2
**Preparation Time:** 20 Minutes

**Ingredients:**
500 ml of freshly juiced tomatoes
(done by you)
1 juiced cucumber
1/4 green pepper
1 stick of celery
1/2 clove of garlic
A few basil leaves
Olive oil

**Instructions:**

**1** Make the tomato and cucumber juice and mix together.

**2** Next finely dice the pepper, garlic and celery and add to the soup mixture.

**3** Tear the basil leaves and stir in and top with olive oil. Season to taste.

**4** Make more tomato-ey or watery by adjusting the tomato and cucumber quantities. For extra sweetness blend with one red pepper.

# Alkalising Raw Soup

High in good fats and also cucumber which is well known for its cleansing properties

**Serves:** 2
**Preparation Time:** 20 Minutes

**Ingredients:**
1 avocado
2 onions
1/2 red or green pepper
1 cucumber
2 handfuls of spinach
1/2 clove of garlic
Bragg Liquid Aminos to taste
100ml of light vegetable Bouillon
(yeast free)
Juice of 1 lemon or lime
Optional: coriander, parsley,
cumin.

**Instructions:**

**1** Blend the avocado and stock to form a light paste, then add the other ingredients and blend.

Simple as that!

# Alkaline Spring-time Soup

This is 100% alkaline, refreshing and filling.

**Serves:** 2
**Preparation Time:** 30 Minutes

**Ingredients:**
1 shallot or small brown onion
1/2 cucumber
1 tablespoon of olive, flax or
Udo's Choice
250ml vegetable stock (yeast free)
2 sprigs of mint
1lb or 450g of frozen peas
1/2 avocado
Salt & pepper to taste

**Instructions:**

**1** Run some warm water over the peas (in a sieve) to soften and slightly defrost, chop the onion into small pieces (or mince in a pestle & mortar) and then place all ingredients into a blender and blend until smooth.

**2** Now either gently heat (not cook) or enjoy cool (or refrigerated on a hot day!)

Simple.

# Alkaline Tom Yum Soup

This is a nice, spicy, Thai soup that really gives you a different flavour to the usual!

**Serves:** 2
**Preparation Time:** 30 Minutes

**Ingredients:**
1 stick of lemongrass
1-2 red chillies
1/2 brown onion cut into large chunks
Small amount, two small strips of Galangal
Similar amount of fresh ginger
2 keffir lime leaves
2 cloves of garlic
2 tomatoes quartered
Handful of coriander
Bragg Liquid Amino's or Soy Sauce (Bragg is more alkaline)
Handful of beansprouts
600ml of vegetable stock (made with vegetable bouillon or yeast-free stock cubes)
As much tofu as you'd like cubed

**Instructions:**

**1** First, prepare all of the flavours. So chop a few thin strips of ginger and galangal, cut the stem from the chilli and bash it with the flat part of the knife (you don't need to chop), cut the lemongrass into 1.5 inch pieces and bash flat.

**2** Bash the garlic and rip the lime leaves into two. You should be salivating at the smell of these flavours by now.

**3** Now, throw those flavoursome pieces into a large pot with the stock and the onion. Once it has come to the boil add the tofu. Two mins later add the tomato and a minute after that add the coriander and beansprouts if you fancy, then remove from the heat and serve immediately.

The soup should be hot and tasty. If you want it sweeter and are happy to be less than 100% alkaline you can add a pinch of brown sugar or palm sugar if you have it. Season with salt and pepper.

I love it without the sugar but hey, you might want to take the edge off the chilli! Enjoy!

# Almond Gazpacho

Gaspacho aux amandes - very exotic and continental! And very tasty!

**Serves:** 4
**Preparation Time:** 30 Minutes

**Ingredients:**
1 cup whole blanched and peeled almonds
2 cups stale bread, cut in cubes, without crust
6 tbsp olive oil
2 cups of water
2 large garlic cloves
1.5 tsp himalayan or sea salt

**Instructions:**

**1** Cover the bread in water in a bowl and leave it to soak for a bit. Now, chuck the almonds, garlic and salt in a food processor and blend it up until it is quite smooth.

**2** Next, go back to your bread and squeeze out the water and put into the blender and blend again until nice and smooth. Now drizzle in the oil (while it is still blending) slow and steady.

**3** Now slowly pour in the water and pulse the blender until it is a nice smooth soup!

Perfect!

P.S. you can garnish with whatever you like - normal gazpacho toppings, or I've found chives, cucumber, spring onions and mint all work well.

# Rice, Tomato & Cumin Soup

This is a filling soup, great for winter and great to transition you to the alkaline diet

**Serves:** 2
**Preparation Time:** 30 Minutes

**Ingredients:**
½ medium onion
2 garlic cloves, crushed
1 tsp of coconut oil
1 tsp ground cumin
85g brown basmati rice
2 tins of chopped tomatoes
290ml yeast free vegetable stock
small bunch parsley, chopped
sea salt and ground black pepper
4 tbsp olive oil

**Instructions:**

**1** Cook the brown rice as per the instructions on the packet. When this has nearly finished cooking, chop all of the vegetables as per the instructions above and then lightly sauté the garlic and onion (but don't let anything go brown!) in a large saucepan with the coconut oil.

**2** Now throw in the cumin and tomatoes, rice and stock and cook for another 6-8 minutes.

**3** Season to taste, add the parsley, serve in nice big bowls and drizzle with olive oil!

# Spicy Alkaline Summer Soup!

Tangy spicy soup that really hits the mark!

**Serves:** 2
**Preparation Time:** 20 Minutes

**Ingredients:**
1 & 1/2 cucumbers
7 tomatoes
3 large handfuls of spinach
1 avocado
1.5 inch chunk of fresh ginger
1 red chilli
250ml vegetable stock (cooled)
1/2 lime or lemon juice
2 tablespoons of olive oil,
avocado oil or Udo's Choice
Salt & pepper to taste

**Instructions:**

**1** Roughly chop the cucumbers, tomatoes, avocado, ginger and chilli.

**2** Now place all of the ingredients in a blender and blend until smooth! If you want to have this soup warm, just warm it gently.

**3** It should never be so hot that you couldn't put your finger in it - so never boil!

# Tuscan Bean Soup

So... fibre + protein + alkaline minerals = winner.

**Serves:** 6
**Preparation Time:** 30 Minutes

**Ingredients:**
2 tbs (30ml) olive oil
1 medium onion, chopped
2 stalks celery, chopped
4 cloves garlic, chopped
3 cups (680g) chopped tomatoes
6 cups (900g) tinned cannelini beans
5 cups (1.25ltr) water
1/2 tsp (3g) Himalayan Salt
Freshly ground pepper, to taste
1 cup (75g) spelt pasta shells, or other small pasta shape
1/4 cup (9g) fresh basil leaves, coarsely chopped

**Instructions:**

**1** Firstly, you need to steam fry the onions, celery, and garlic until tender. Do this in a few spoons of water in a large pan.

**2** Once it is all nice and tender you can add the chopped tomatoes (juice n' all) and warm this over a medium to low heat, breaking up the tomatoes so that it is all chunked down in nice small pieces. Cook this together for about fifteen to twenty minutes until everything is infused together.

**3** Now you can add the lovely creamy-textured cannelini beans (drained and rinsed), the water, salt, pepper and cook over a medium-low heat for another twenty minutes.

**4** Once the beans are soft you're good. Now you can add the spelt pasta and cook for another ten to fifteen minutes until it is al dente.

**5** Once the soup has cooled a little bit, stir in the olive oil and add the basil leaves.

This soup rocks, I urge you to try it!

# Classic Carrot & Coriander Soup

This classic soup is always a winner!

**Serves:** 2
**Preparation Time:** 30 Minutes

**Ingredients:**
Coconut Oil
1 onion, chopped
2 garlic cloves, chopped
4 carrots, peeled and chopped
400ml yeast free vegetable stock
3 tbsp chopped fresh coriander
Celtic sea salt
Freshly ground black pepper

**Instructions:**

**1** Gently soften the garlic and onions by lightly frying in a pan with the coconut oil. It will smell coconutty and tropical but it is tasteless. Don't cook it too high and fry until the onion is soft. Don't let the garlic burn!

**2** Now add the chopped carrots and soften those too for 3-4 minutes.

**3** Add the vegetable stock and bring it to the boil. Once boiling reduce the heat to a simmer and cook until the carrots are tender. Don't overcook or you'll lose nutritional value

**4** Now throw in the coriander, salt and pepper. Remove from the heat and blend to your desired consistency.

**5** Optional: you can add a little ginger before blending or chilli if, like me, you love the heat!

# Sweet Red Pepper & Tomato Raw Soup

This is SO quick and easy you'll wonder how you ever coped without it!

**Serves:** 2
**Preparation Time:** 30 Minutes

**Ingredients:**
10 decent sized tomatoes
2 large sweet pointed peppers or
3 normal peppers
1 brown or red onion
2 cloves of garlic
75ml of vegetable stock

**Instructions:**

**1** Bring a little stock to the boil (50ml) in a small frying pan and steam fry the onion and garlic (roughly chopped) for 1-2 minutes.

**2** Now put the rest of the ingredients into the blender with the onion, garlic and remaining stock and blend until smooth. Season and you're done!

Brilliant all year round, but especially good in the sunshine.

# Bibi's Carrot & Butternut Squash Soup

Warm, delicious and unique. Bibi's spicy soup is getting rave reviews on the blog!

**Serves:** 2
**Preparation Time:** 30 Minutes

**Ingredients:**
1 medium sized butternut squash
or pumpkin
2 large carrots
1 large red onion
2-3 garlic cloves
1 fresh red chilli
1 piece of ginger
1.2 litres of veg. stock (yeast free)
Juice of 1 orange (optional)
Fresh thyme leaves
Salt and pepper
Olive/Coconut oil

**Instructions:**

**1** First up, you need to cut the onion and garlic cloves into nice fine pieces. Now get going on the squash by peeling it and cutting it into cube sized pieces the size of a standard dice. Peel the carrots and cut a similar size.

**2** Now, carefully deseed the chilli and cut it into small pieces. Wash your hands thoroughly now, before you wipe your eyes, put them down your pants etc. Peel the ginger and chop roughly.

**3** Now the cooking starts. Heat the oil (coconut is preferable) in a large pot and gently fry the onion and garlic on a low heat until they begin to soften (approx 4 min). Throw in the carrot and squash and season and then fry for another 5-6 minutes until it all starts to soften a little. Add more oil if you need it here.

**4** Add 1.2 litres of organic/yeast free vegetable stock, the ginger, chilli and thyme leaves. Bring it all to the boil and then simmer for about 25 min until the squash and carrots are soft.

**5** Now is the fun part - throw it all into a blender and puree it up until it is smooth (or slightly chunky like in the picture - this is how I (Ross) prefer my soups!)

**6** If you're looking for an extra zing you can now squeeze in fresh juice from 1 orange - but this does decrease the alkalising effect of the soup a little. Delicious though.

# Spinach & Courgette Alkaline Soup

The fusion of flavours in this totally alkaline raw soup is amazing - you have to try it!

**Serves:** 2
**Preparation Time:** 15 Minutes

**Ingredients:**
2 spring onions
1 medium courgette/zucchini
1 avocado
500ml vegetable stock
1/2 tin cannellini or butter beans
4 big handfuls of baby spinach
1/2 lemon, juiced
4 tsp. finely chopped mint leaves
1/2 garlic clove, chopped
Freshly ground black pepper
Sea or Himalayan salt

**Optional:**

For a different variety of tastes, you can add rocket leaves or watercress too.

### Instructions:

**1** Firstly, prepare all of your vegetables by chopping them roughly so that they can be blended.

**2** Next add 50ml of stock to the blender along with your avocado and blend this until smooth.

**3** Now throw in the spinach and courgette, the beans (drained and rinsed), garlic and as much stock as you feel to make the soup the consistency you want it.

**4** Now add the mint, salt and pepper, squeeze over the lemon juice and enjoy!

# Alkalising Cucumber & Watercress Soup

Fast, filling and highly alkaline raw soup

**Serves:** 2
**Preparation Time:** 30 Minutes

**Ingredients:**
1/2 bunch of spring onions, chopped
1 large cucumber, deseeded and chopped
2 bunches of watercress (or as much as you like, to taste, keep adding more and more if you like!)
1¾ pint water yeast free vegetable stock (cooled)
(Himalayan) Salt and freshly ground black pepper

**Instructions:**

**1**  Chop, slice and dice all of the ingredients and place in a blender.

**2**  Make the stock by putting a small amount of hot water onto the stock cube or bouillon and once melted, top up with cold water.

**3**  Add this to the blender too and then blend it all up! Serve chilled with an ice cube per bowl.

# Salad

It is no surprise that salads are some of the most important meals on the alkaline diet. You can have salads as a stand alone meal or as a side and they are a fantastic way of boosting your alkaline veggie consumption.

I certainly advocate you getting into the habit of having a salad (however small) with every meal, as you're getting a great hit of raw, alkaline goodness.

You can mix and match these salads and pump any of them up with the addition of tofu, beans, pulses and nuts.

# Spinach Salad

A simple, highly alkaline salad that is tasty any time, any place!

**Serves:** 3-4
**Preparation Time:** 10 Minutes

**Ingredients:**
1 large bag (250g) of fresh baby spinach
1 handful rocket (optional)
1/2 red onion
1/2 chopped avocado
Juice of 1/2 lemon
Avocado or olive oil
Himalayan salt & black pepper

**Instructions:**

**1** Thoroughly wash all of the leaves and place in a large salad bowl.

**2** Thinly slice the red onion, chop the avocado and mix into the leaves. Be reasonably rough with the avocado so it becomes a part of the dressing and partly coats the leaves.

**3** Squeeze the lemon juice over the salad and drizzle with oil. Season to taste.

Serves 2 as a main meal or 4 as a side.

# Fill-You-Up Alkaline Salad

Another highly alkaline salad that will keep you going for hours and hours!

**Serves:** 3-4
**Preparation Time:** 10 Minutes

**Ingredients:**
2 Handfuls of baby spinach
1 Handful of rocket leaves
1 Handful of cos lettuce
1 Handful of lamb's lettuce
100g tofu
1 serve of quinoa
½ can of chickpeas
1 avocado
1 handful of seeds & nuts
6 cherry tomatoes
½ cucumber
½ green or red pepper
Olive oil (& coconut oil)
Lemon
Himalayan salt & black pepper

**Instructions:**

**1** Lightly fry off the tofu in coconut oil (coconut is the only safe oil to cook with) and make the quinoa to the packet's instructions (usually 1 part quinoa, 2 parts water, boiled and then simmered until the water evaporates, about 10 minutes).

**2** Now prepare the salad by washing everything thoroughly and chopping to how you like it. I prefer to rip my salad leaves – makes it more rustic (note: use whatever leaves you have)

**3** Mix everything together including the nuts and seeds (I used sesame, pumpkin and sunflower seeds with a few almonds) with the juice of half a lemon and a drizzle of olive, hemp, avocado or Udo's Choice oil and serve.

**4** Feel full and happy.

# Herb Salad

A tasty salad, characterised by the wonderfully fragrant coriander

**Serves:** 3-4
**Preparation Time:** 10 Minutes

**Ingredients:**
Lambs leaf lettuce
Romaine (cos) lettuce
Handful of baby spinach leaves
Fresh coriander
Fresh parsley
Fennel
2 spring onions
1/2 lemon juice
Olive oil

**Instructions:**

**1** Pick as much lettuce as you feel you need.

**2** Thoroughly wash the lettuce leaves and spinach and tear the lettuce leaves to make mouthful sized shapes.

**3** Wash and thinly slice the spring onion and then wash and roughly chop the herbs.

**4** Mix all ingredients together and dress with lemon juice and olive oil.

# Coleslaw Zing!

A brilliant, tasty side-dish or a salad in its own right

**Serves:** 2
**Preparation Time:** 15 Minutes

**Ingredients:**
Half red cabbage
Half green cabbage
1 carrot
1 courgette
Handful of parsley
1/2 lime
1 small chilli (optional)
2 tbsp of olive/avocado oil or
Udo's Choice
Himalayan salt

**Instructions:**

**1**  Thinly slice or shred the cabbage, carrot and courgette.

**2**  Mix with parsley, lime juice, thinly sliced chilli, oil and salt.

**3**  Refrigerate and serve!

# Tabbouleh

A Moroccan, alkaline, super-salad

**Serves:** 2
**Preparation Time:** 20 Minutes

**Ingredients:**
2 tomatoes
1 bunch spring onions
1/2 cucumber
Sesame seeds
1 handful of mint
2 large handfuls of parsley
1 lemon (juiced)
Olive/avocado oil or Udo's Choice
Himalayan salt & black pepper

**Instructions:**

**1** Finely chop and combine all ingredients, mixing well and adding more lemon juice if necessary.

**2** Leave, refrigerated for an hour or so for the flavours to infuse and serve!

# Warm Broccoli & Tomato Salad

A filling salad, this makes an excellent lunch or main dinner

**Serves:** 2
**Preparation Time:** 15 Minutes

**Ingredients:**
2 serves of wild rice (or brown)
1 pepper
Large handful of beansprouts
4 broccoli florets
1 lime or lemon
Handful of cabbage
6 mini tomatoes
Olive/avocado/flax oil or Udo's Choice

**Instructions:**

**1** Cook the wild rice according to the instructions and lightly steam the broccoli and cabbage.

**2** Thinly slice the pepper, half the tomatoes, and place on top of the rice alongside the broccoli and beansprouts.

**3** Top with the lemon/lime juice or olive oil. Add chopped spinach leaves for a more alkalising meal!

# Broad Bean Salad with Tumeric Potatoes

A sexy salad for the summer months! The different textures and flavours work brilliantly together.

**Serves:** 2
**Preparation Time:** 25 Minutes

**Ingredients:**
5 tbsp coconut oil (or olive)
85g broad beans
½ onion, sliced
A handful of cherry tomatoes
Pinch of sea or Himalayan salt
100g new potatoes, sliced rough
1 tsp turmeric
1 handful each of parsley, basil
and chives all chopped

**Instructions:**

**1** Firstly, heat two tablespoons of coconut oil in a pan and lightly fry the broad beans and onion for about two minutes. If you don't have coconut oil, you can use olive oil but I do highly recommend coconut as this is the only oil that is healthy to cook with.

**2** Take the beans and onions off the heat and let them cool down a little

**3** Chop the cherry tomatoes in half and sprinkle with salt and drizzle with olive oil and then leave to one side.

**4** Next you need to parboil the new potatoes. Put them in a pan of boiling water and add the tumeric to the pan. Boil for eight minutes and then drain. Now fry these in more coconut oil for another five minutes to make healthy chunky chip slices.

**5** To serve, mix the potato, broad beans and tomato together in a bowl with the herbs, drizzle with olive oil and season to taste.

# Carrot & Almond Salad

A highly nutritious and crunchy salad. Love the texture!

**Serves:** 2
**Preparation Time:** 20 Minutes

**Ingredients:**
1 carrot
1/4 red cabbage
2 spring onions
Handful of baby spinach leaves
Handful of almonds, sliced
1 clove of garlic
1/4 grapefruit
1/2 lemon
Olive oil

**Instructions:**

**1** Thinly slice the cabbage and slice the carrot to make rounds.

**2** Cut the spring onions lengthways and then half to create shreds and peel the grapefruit and chop into chunks

**3** Crush the garlic and mix all ingredients together. Dress with lemon and olive oil or any other dressing from this book.

# Brown Rice Salad

A salad with warmth, substance and oodles of taste!

**Serves:** 2
**Preparation Time:** 25 Minutes

**Ingredients:**
1 serve of brown rice
4 cups broccoli florets
2 cups cherry tomatoes, halved
2 big handfuls of spinach
1 big handful of rocket
1/2 avocado
1/2 cucumber, diced
Juice of 1 lemon
1 tablespoon olive oil
2 tsp dried oregano

**Instructions:**

**1** Cook the brown rice to the packet instructions and then very lightly stream the broccoli, until it is just tender.

**2** Now mix all of the ingredients into a bowl, stirring in the lemon and olive oil.

**3** Season lightly and serve while the broccoli is still warm.

# Snow-Pea & Asparagus Salad

The contrasting textures of the snowpeas and the asparagus is just fantastic. A real treat!

**Serves:** 2
**Preparation Time:** 15 Minutes

**Ingredients:**
2 cups snowpeas/mange tout
1 bunch fresh asparagus
1/2 packet fresh bean sprouts
1 cup spinach
Sprinkling of pine nuts or
chopped almonds
Cold pressed olive oil

**Instructions:**

**1** Very lightly steam the asparagus and snow peas, for 3-6 minutes.

**2** Let these ingredients cool slightly while you mix all of the other ingredients into a large bowl.

**3** Now add in the asparagus and snow peas and season lightly. As an option squeeze fresh lemon or lime juice over the salad and serve!

# Tangy Sprout Salad

You can play around with this salad and mix it up a bit, but the dressing is to die for!

**Serves:** 2
**Preparation Time: 10** Minutes

**Ingredients:**
1/2 Cucumber
8 Cherry tomatoes
2 Handfuls spinach leaves
Handful lettuce leaves
1/2 Can chickpeas
2 Large handfuls of sprouts
- I suggest alfalfa, broccoli and mung bean

Dressing:

1 tsp Braggs Liquid Aminos (preferable, but soy sauce if not available)
1 tbsp olive oil
1 inch of fresh ginger, grated
1 tbsp of orange rind
1 tsp of lime rind
1/2 lime juice

**Instructions:**

**1** Prepare and mix all of the dressing ingredients (with a little water if it is too strong).

**2** Cut the cucumber into matchsticks and half the cherry tomatoes.

**3** Roughly tear the lettuce leaves and drain & rinse the chickpeas. Now mix all of the ingredients together in a large bowl!

Enjoy!

# Warm Baby Potato & Asparagus Salad

Delicious, summery and filling.  Exactly how I like my salads!

**Serves:** 2
**Preparation Time:** 10 Minutes

**Ingredients:**
350g baby new potatoes
Handul of walnuts, chopped
1 bunch asparagus
2 handfuls of spinach
3 large radishes, sliced
1 large beetroot
1 can of mixed beans

For the dressing

50ml olive oil
2 tbsp lemon juice
Optional splash of Bragg Liquid
Aminos

**Instructions:**

**1** Pre-heat oven to 200C/Gas 6 & then parboil the potatoes for 15 minutes until slightly tender. Drain and cool for 5 minutes before putting in a roasting pan.

**2** Now make the alkaline dressing: mix together all the dressing ingredients, seasoning with salt and pepper if desired.

**3** Now roast the potatoes for about 25 minutes, until soft on the inside and crisp on the outside. Sprinkle the walnuts on a separate baking tray and dry roast for 3 - 4 minutes to intensify their flavour. Do not let them burn!

**4** Trim the woody ends off the asparagus spears and discard. Steam the asparagus for 5 to 7 minutes (depending on size) until tender.

**5** To assemble the salad: cover the base of a large, wide salad bowl with spinach leaves; sit the potatoes on top followed by the chopped radish, sliced beetroot and mixed beans (drained and rinsed).   Now pour over the dressing and enjoy!

# Power Salad

This salad never fails to deliver. Filling, tasty, alkaline and always fits the bill.

**Serves:** 2
**Preparation Time:** 10 Minutes

**Ingredients:**
1 can of chickpeas
1 stick of celery
Baby spinach leaves
Romaine lettuce leaves
3 roma tomatoes
1 red pepper
1 avocado
1 bunch asparagus
1 lemon (juice for dressing)
Olive/avocado/flax oil or Udo's Choice

**Instructions:**

**1** Chop and mix all of the ingredients in a large bowl, allowing the avocado to mash up and coat the salad. Be sure to drain and rinse the chickpeas and wash everything thoroughly.

# Warm Lentil Salad

A filling, warming and satisfying salad - all year 'round. Enjoy!

**Serves:** 2
**Preparation Time:** 10 Minutes

**Ingredients:**
150g of dried lentils or 1 can of prepared (if you're in a hurry)
400ml Vegetable bouillon, yeast-free
½ lemon
2 garlic cloves
1 onion
1 pepper/capsicum
4 tomatoes, skinned
1 inch of fresh ginger
1 courgette/zucchini
A handful of basil or coriander
A sprinkle of seeds
A little coconut oil

**Instructions:**

**1** First up, get the lentils cooked by simmering in the veggie stock with the ½ lemon squeezed in. Simmer for about half an hour, topping up with more stock if it boils away.

**2** Then very gently soften the onion in a frying pan, using coconut oil. Coconut oil is the only oil that does not become toxic when exposed to heat, light or air. If you don't have coconut oil you can steam fry in a little stock, or if you don't believe me then you can use olive oil!

**3** Once the onion is softened, you should add the courgette, garlic and peppers stirring until these have softened too. Don't let anything get too soft though, you still want a little crunch. Now add the tomatoes and ginger and cook until warmed through.

**4** Now simply stir in the lentils, herbs and seeds, seasoning to taste and you're done!

Serve either beside or on top of the leaves and voila, a lovely alkaline meal!

# Gigantic Kale Salad

Kale is very alkalising and this salad is a real treat.  The variety of flavours is amazing!

**Serves:** 2
**Preparation Time:** 30 Minutes

**Ingredients:**
1 big bunch of Kale
2 carrots
2 handfuls of cherry/baby plum tomatoes
1 lemon, juiced
½ cup soaked pine nuts
¼ cup of sesame seeds
1 medium red onion
Raw black olives
1/4 cup of olive/avocado oil or Udo's Choice
A pinch of Himalayan salt
A few dashes of Bragg Liquid Aminos or pHlavor Salt Spray
A pinch of black pepper

**Optional:**

Sun-dried tomatoes
Goat's cheese

## Instructions:

**1** This is a totally raw, quick dish – so get ready and let's rock! Firstly, shred the kale so that it is nice and fine, grate the carrots and cut the tomatoes in half.

**2** Now slice up the onion quite thin and half the olives (make sure there are no seeds in the olives).

**3** Now mix into a large bowl with everything else!  Season, serve and enjoy.

If you are transitioning you can also add some sun-dried or semi-dried tomatoes, goats cheese etc to this recipe, but to be honest it is delicious enough as it is!

Enjoy as a main in itself or as a salad alongside your main dish.

# Carrot & Courgette Stack

Raw, fresh and alkaline - this is a vibrant, refreshing lunch or dinner

**Serves:** 2
**Preparation Time:** 20 Minutes

**Ingredients:**
2 serves quinoa
Handful baby spinach leaves
1 carrot
1 courgette
1/2 avocado
Sesame seeds
1 lemon or lime
Olive/avocado oil or Udo's Choice

**Instructions:**

**1** Cook the quinoa and arrange a base on two plates.

**2** Grate the carrot and courgette to form a stack.

**3** Sprinkle chopped spinach and avocado on top and then top with sesame seeds, lemon juice and oil.

Season to taste.

# Bright & Breezy Salad

Delicious, highly alkalising, raw, crisp and an easy way to get a big hit of veggies

**Serves:** 2
**Preparation Time:** 30 Minutes

**Ingredients:**
1 bunch of parsley
1 handful of coriander
1 small red onion
2 red peppers/capsicums
1 cucumber
1 small can of sweetcorn
2 celery stalks
1 carrot

**Optional dressing:**
Juice of 1 lemon
20ml olive oil
1 clove of garlic, minced

**Instructions:**

**1**  Finely chop the parsley and roughly chop the coriander. Now dice the red onion, peppers, cucumber and celery.

**2**  Grate the carrot and throw it all in together with the sweetcorn into a giant bowl and mix with your hands.

**3**  You can dress with lemon juice, olive oil and garlic or use our garlic dressing or another dressing from this cook book!

Enjoy!

# Dinners & Main Meals

These alkaline meals have been designed to be warming, satisfying and to feel like a treat - no matter how healthy they sneakily are!

These are my core main meals, my armoury of dinners that I know I can always cook quickly and easily and with pretty much the same stock ingredients.

The more you get used to the recipes, the more you can adapt them and you get faster and faster at preparing them!

These are all alkaline, tasty and easy. Enjoy!

# Chilli-Lime Steam Fry

Vibrant, fruity, healthy and quick main meal. What more could you ask for?

**Serves:** 2
**Preparation Time:** 25 Minutes

**Ingredients:**
Small block ginger
1 garlic clove
Bok-choi or other Asian greens
Beansprouts
1 carrot
5 spring onions
1 pepper
1/2 courgette
4 broccoli florets
Handful sugar-snap peas
1 teaspoon vegetable bouillon
or half a stock cub
(yeast and salt-free)
Soba noodles or brown rice

**Dressing:**
1 small red chilli
(or as hot as you can handle!)
Large handful of coriander
Juice of 1 lime

**Instructions:**

**1** First, finely chop the chilli and pick the coriander leaves. Now with a pestle and mortar mash together and add the lime juice. Leave to one side to infuse.

**2** Now get the rice cooking if you're having rice. If you're having soba noodles you can get these ready at the same time as you do step four.

**3** Finely slice the carrots into matchsticks, slice the bok choi, finely slice the spring onion, and dice the pepper and courgette.

**4** Cut the broccoli florets so they are quite small too. We are aiming to make the food sliced to cook quickly.

**5** Prepare the stock with 50ml of water and heat in a frying pan until boiling. Next steam fry the garlic and ginger for a minute before adding the remaining vegetables.

**6** After three minutes of steam frying. Remove and place on a bed of brown rice or soba noodles. Coat with chilli-lime dressing and serve

# Alkaline Chilli-non-Carne

Another excellent alkaline meal that is filling, easy and tasty!

**Serves:** 2
**Preparation Time:** 40 Minutes

**Ingredients:**
1 tbsp olive oil
1 onion, chopped
1 garlic clove, crushed
1 can chopped tomatoes
2 tbsp tomato puree
1 red chillies, thinly sliced,
(or 3-4 tsp dried chilli flakes)
1/2 tsp ground cumin
1/2 tsp ground coriander
Bragg Liquid Aminos
1/2 yeast free veg stock cube
Himalayan Salt and freshly
ground black pepper
200g can red kidney beans,
drained
1 head of broccoli, chopped sma
1 small handful of spinach
Wedges of lime, to serve

**Instructions:**

**1** Heat 50ml of water or stock in a large, heavy-based saucepan and steam fry the onion and garlic until softened.

**2** Stir in the chopped tomatoes, tomato puree, fresh chilli or chilli flakes, cumin, ground coriander, and Bragg Liquid Aminos sauce and crumble in the stock cube.

**3** Season well with salt and pepper. Bring to a simmer, cover with a lid and cook over a gentle heat for about 20 minutes stirring occasionally until the mixture is rich and thickened.

**4** Add the kidney beans and fresh coriander. Cook for a further eight minutes, uncovered, before removing from the heat, adding any extra seasoning if necessary.

**5** Leave to cool slightly and add in raw, finely chopped broccoli and spinach; and add some avocado or olive oil.

This is ideal served with lime wedges and also rice, guacamole (or just mashed avocado) and a big green salad.

# Tania's Lemon-y Pasta Sensation!

It is alkaline, filling, delicious and very, very quick.

**Serves:** 2
**Preparation Time:** 10 Minutes

**Ingredients:**
Spelt pasta (enough for 2)
1 small broccoli head
Handful of peas
2 garlic cloves
1 small courgette
1 tomato
1/2 red onion
2 handfuls of rocket and/or
spinach (and any other greens)
Juice of 1 lemon
1 teaspoon of coconut oil
Drizzle of olive oil
Himalayan salt & black pepper to
taste

**Instructions:**

**1** Firstly, get the pasta on the go. Then chop all of the greens to a size and shape you like and very lightly fry the broccoli, peas, garlic, red onion and courgette in the coconut oil.

**2** Once the pasta is ready, drain and put into the pan with the greens, add the chopped tomato and rocket and stir in the lemon.

**3** When you're ready to serve, put it all in a bowl and drizzle with olive oil and season.

Optional: I love chilli so I usually add some at the end. Nice, fresh and hot!

Enjoy!

# Alkaline Veggie Fajitas

One of the world's easiest and most popular dishes made alkaline!

**Serves:** 2
**Preparation Time:** 40 Minutes

**Ingredients:**
Wheat-free tortillas
1 avocado
Handful of spinach
Broccoli florets
1 grated carrot
Lettuce leaves
Olive oil
Pine nuts
Tomato
Red onion
Paprika
Coriander

**Optional:**
1/2 tin of kidney beans
1/2 block of firm tofu

**Instructions:**

**1** To make a salsa, finely chop the tomato and red onion and mix in a bowl with a little olive oil.

**2** Finely chop and lightly steam the broccoli and then mash and spread the avocado and salsa into the wrap.

If using the kidney beans, gently warm in a pan and mash a little.

**3** Add grated carrot, pine nuts, leaves, herbs and spices and optional kidney beans to the wrap and roll over.

**Note:** to make it even more filling, you can add some firm tofu that has been lightly fried in coconut oil.

# Aubergine & Chick Pea Balti

Britain's favourite dish made alkaline!  Being a Brummie for 8yrs gave me a fine appreciate of the Balti!

**Serves:** 2
**Preparation Time:** 10 Minutes

**Ingredients:**
2 tbsp coconut oil
1 onion, peeled and finely sliced
1/2 tsp cumin seeds
1 aubergine
1 potato
1 tin chickpeas
1 tsp ground coriander
1/2 tsp ground cumin
1/4 tsp turmeric
Fresh coriander

**Sauce:**

2 tbsp coconut oil
1 onion, peeled and finely sliced
2 cloves garlic, crushed
2 tsp ginger, peeled and grated
6 whole cloves
450g plum tomatoes
1/4 tsp turmeric
1/2 tsp ground coriander
1/2 tsp ground cumin
1 1/2 tsp salt
1 tsp red chilli powder, to taste

**Instructions:**

**1** Firstly, for the vegetables, warm the coconut oil and cook the onion and cumin seeds for about two minutes, until it all starts getting a little bit fragrant.

**2** Next, put in the chopped potato, aubergine, chickpeas, ground coriander, cumin and turmeric. Cook again for three minutes and then put aside.

**3** Now it is time to make the sauce.  Warm a little more coconut oil in the pan, add the onion, garlic, ginger and cloves and quickly cook for sixty seconds before throwing in the chopped tomatoes, tumeric and other spices and savouries.  Get this really going for about three minutes.

**4** Get a hand blender (or big blender) and roughly blend the sauces.  Then add the vegetables in (but don't blend), the coriander, water and any further needed salt and pepper.

**5** Simmer away for twenty minutes and then you're ready to serve. Sprinkle some fresh coriander on top to finish and serve with brown rice!

# Aubergine & Black Bean Alkaline Chilli

A variation on the original chilli recipe - this one is a twist on the Central American style!

**Serves:** 2
**Preparation Time:** 35 minutes
**Ingredients:**
Coconut or olive oil
200g aubergine cut into cubes
1 red onion, finely chopped
2 garlic cloves, crushed
5 small red chillies, chopped OR
A dozen dried chillies
400g can of tomtoes (organic)
1/2 tsp ground coriander
Pinch of ground cumin
Pinch of ground cinnamon
250g cooked black beans
Sea salt
Freshly ground black pepper

**Optional:**
2 serves of brown rice, quinoa or cous cous

## Instructions:

**1** Firstly, if you are preparing the black beans yourself, follow the packet guides to get these cooked. If you are using tinned then drain and rinse these before cooking.

**2** Chop all of the ingredients as suggested above. The aubergine cubes should be about 1.5cm on each side. You can de seed the chilli if you don't like it too hot!

**3** Next, heat the coconut oil in a pan. Please try to use coconut oil - all other oils become toxic when heated. If you don't have coconut oil, use olive this time - but then invest in coconut!

**4** Now fry the aubergines for about four minutes, to colour and soften. Remove, drain and dry on some kitchen paper towel.

**5** Now soften the onions and garlic in the same pan and add the chillies and cook for just a couple of minutes. After this, throw in the tomatoes, coriander, and spices and the dried aubergine and let this simmer away for about five or six minutes.

**6** Finally add the black beans (prepared yourself according to the packet instructions or tinned) and leave to simmer for another ten minutes - and at this time cook the brown rice/quinoa or cous cous.

# Alkaline Cous Cous

Easy, filling and mostly raw alkaline cous-cous. This one is a life save!

**Serves:** 2
**Preparation Time:** 15 Minutes

**Ingredients:**
2 servings of cous cous
(according to packet)
1 handful spinach
2 tomatoes
1 avocado
1/2 chopped pepper
Seasonal herbs
Juice of 1 lemon or lime
Olive/avocado oil or Udo's Choice

**Instructions:**

**1**  Cook cous cous according to the packet instructions.

**2**  Chop the pepper, tomatoes, avocado, spinach and herbs and place over cous cous. Drizzle with oil and lime/lemon juice.

**3**  Optional: to make more substantial add lightly steamed green vegetables such as broccoli, fine beans, sugar snap peas etc.

# Thai Green curry Made Alkaline

My absolute favourite!

**Serves:** 2
**Preparation Time:** 40 Minutes

**Ingredients:**
2 spring onions
Broccoli
1/4 cauliflower
1 carrot sliced
125ml coconut milk
Handful of coriander
Large finger of ginger
1 stick of lemongrass
1-2 chillies
2 limes
Asian greens (bok choi etc)
1 teaspoon of green curry paste
Cubes of firm tofu (optional)
Soba noodles or brown rice.

**Instructions:**

**1** Juice the lime, slice and bash the lemongrass and chilli, slice the ginger and roughly chop the coriander. Mix together and allow to infuse.

**2** Next thinly slice the spring onion and carrot, cut the broccoli and cauliflower and steam fry along with the Asian greens and tofu if desired.

**3** Once steamed (five mins) add the infused chilli, lime and lemon-grass, coconut milk and paste.

**4** Gently simmer for five minutes and serve either alone or with soba noodles or brown ice.

Optional: grate the lime before juicing and use as a garnish when serving.

# Alkaline Lunchtime Wraps

Another lifesaver, these are quick, filling, flexible and easy as well as being alkaline!

**Serves:** 2
**Preparation Time:** 10 Minutes

**Ingredients:**
1/3 cucumber
1 tomato
Lettuce leaves
Small handful spinach leaves
Sunflower seeds
Hummous
Wheat free tortillas/wraps
1/4 lemon

**Instructions:**

**1**  Wash salad items thoroughly and dice to enable easy wrapping!

**2**  Spread hummous along the wrap, just left of centre.

**3**  Sprinkle the seeds onto the hummous (it makes them stick so they don't fall out) and then place the salad ingredients into the wrap.

**4**  Wrap up by folding over the bottom length first ( to prevent spill-age) and then wrapping over, tucking it in tight.

# Spicy Carrot & Greens

A raw, crunchy alkaline meal in minutes

**Serves:** 2
**Preparation Time:** 15 Minutes

**Ingredients:**
1 large broccoli
2 carrots
6 brussels sprouts
2 cloves of garlic
1 tsp of caraway seeds
1/2 lemon
Peel of 1 lemon
Olive oil

**Instructions:**

**1** Slice the carrot and thinly slice the brussels and chop the broccoli. Lightly steam the vegetables for 5-8 minutes.

**2** When this has finished steaming, chop the garlic and warm gently in a pan with the caraway seeds, lemon peel, juice of 1/2 lemon and the olive oil.

**3** Once it has warmed for a minute or so add the carrot and Brussels and mix.

# Almost Alkaline Lasagne

Just as tasty as normal lasagne but ten-times more healthy!

**Serves:** 2
**Preparation Time:** 60 Minutes

**Ingredients:**
Spelt Lasagne
2 large handfuls of baby spinach
1 pack (500g) soft silken tofu
1 large aubergine
1 courgette
8 roma tomatoes
Handful of fresh basil
1 red pepper
1 lemon
2 garlic cloves
1 small red onion

**Instructions:**

**1** Preheat your oven to 180 degrees. Peel the red pepper by grilling until it is starting to burn, then placing on a plate and covering with cling film. After a few minutes remove the cling film and lift away the peel.

**2** Next, peel 4 tomatoes by placing them in a bowl of boiling water for 1-2 minutes. Lift the tomatoes out one-by-one and slice gently through the skin with a sharp knife. The skin should come away.

**3** Blend the pepper, tomatoes, one clove of garlic and basil to form a sauce and set to one side.

**4** Now, blend the tofu, the other garlic clove and the juice of the lemon to form a paste and then blend in the spinach to form a second sauce.

**5** Grill the aubergine and courgette until almost cooked and then remove from the grill, sprinkle with a little salt and leave for 5 minutes. After this time is up, pat gently to remove excess moisture. The lasagne will become too sloppy if this step is missed.

**6** Slice the remaining four tomatoes and layer with the aubergine and courgette, cover with some of the tofu and spinach mix and then a layer of lasagne. Repeat until you are at the top of the dish and then pour over the tomato and pepper sauce. Cook for 35-40 minutes and serve with a fresh, green salad.

# Vegetable Alkaline Pasta

Basic pasta dish for healthy, alkaline fast food

**Serves:** 2
**Preparation Time:** 20 Minutes

**Ingredients:**
1/2 pack of vegetable or spelt pasta
1 courgette
1 medium broccoli
5 garlic gloves
4 tomatoes
Handful of basil leaves
1 tbsp. olive oil
Chillies, thinly sliced, to taste
Himalayan salt and black pepper.

**Instructions:**

**1** Cook the pasta, stir in olive oil and leave to one side. Now, on a low, gentle heat, warm the oil and slowly cook the garlic, basil and chilli for two minutes.

**2** Next add the remaining vegetables, sliced to make it small and quick to cook.

**3** Mix everything together including the pasta and stir for two more minutes.

**4** Season to taste and serve. If you love garlic then you can even omit the stage of cooking it with the chilli, and simply add raw, sliced thinly.

# Rice Paper Rolls

Can be a starter or a stand-alone meal

**Serves:** 2
**Preparation Time:** 20 Minutes

**Ingredients:**
Rice paper ( uncooked)
1/2 cucumber
Handful of beansprouts
Handful of other sprouts
4 spring onions
Handful coriander
1 carrot
Bragg Liquid Aminos
1 chilli

**Instructions:**

**1** Slice the carrot and cucumber into matchsticks and slice the spring onion lengthways and half (to make it appear shredded).

**2** 'Cook' the rice paper rolls by filling a large bowl with hot water submerging the rice paper until it becomes pliable.

**3** Roughly chop the coriander and arrange all ingredients into the rice paper rolls.

**4** Dress with Bragg Liquid Aminos and roll.

# Basic Alkaline 'Stir' Fry

Simple, straight forward meal for those nights where you need something easy without having to think!

**Serves:** 2
**Preparation Time:** 20 Minutes

**Ingredients:**
4 broccoli florets
4 cauliflower florets
1 pepper
Handful beansprouts
Handful alfalfa/mung bean sprouts
3 spring onions
1 garlic clove, chopped
Bragg Liquid Aminos
Wild/brown basmati rice

**Instructions:**

**1** Cook rice with yeast-free vegetable stock.

**2** Put a small amount of water in a frying pan and bring to boil.

**3** Steam fry the garlic and onion for three minutes.

**4** Add remaining ingredients and cook for just a few minutes (so it is still crunchy, but warmed)

# Creamy Zucchini Pasta

This pasta dish is so flippin' alkaline and is a great way to hide veggies in a meal for the kids!

**Serves:** 4
**Preparation Time:** 20 Minutes

**Ingredients:**
1 zucchini (courgette)
1 bag of rocket (200g)
1/2 red onion
1 bunch asparagus
12 basil leaves
4 tomatoes
2 cloves garlic
4 serves of spelt or vegetable pasta
Olive oil
Optional Udo's for the sauce

**Instructions:**

**1** Start by getting the pasta boiling, once it is ready, remove from the heat and drain to ensure it doesn't go sticky or soggy. Drizzle it with olive oil if it looks like it might stick together and form one giant pasta shape. At the same time prepare the asparagus by gently steaming for 5-6 minutes.

**2** While this is cooking away, finely dice the red onion and chop the tomato into chunks. Put these to one side with a few handfuls of rocket.

**3** Now it is time to prepare the sauce - so put 1 chopped up zucchini/courgette, the remaining rocket, the basil and the garlic into a blender with a good drizzle of olive or Udo's oil and blend until it becomes a thick, light green sauce. Salt and pepper to taste.

**4** Now, stir the sauce in with the pasta (lightly warm if you like, but don't cook!), put into bowls, top with the tomato, red onion, asparagus and rocket and voila.

A totally raw, alkaline, filling pasta! Brilliant!

# Tomato & Shallot Spaghetti

Another alkaline pasta dish, using lots of raw ingredients to complement the cooked pasta

**Serves:** 4
**Preparation Time:** 20 Minutes

**Ingredients:**
1 tbsp olive oil/coconut oil
½ shallot, finely chopped
1 garlic clove, finely chopped
125g sun-blushed tomatoes, chopped
Handful of cauliflower, chopped small
Large handful of spinach
Large handful of rocket
Handful each chives, parsley, basil, chopped
½ lemon, juice only
250g spelt or wheat free spaghetti, cooked

**Instructions:**

**1** Prepare the pasta according to the packet guidelines (spelt, kamut and wheat free pastas all have different cooking times). While this is cooking away, prepare your vegetables.

**2** Chop the cauliflower so that it is quite tiny, finely chop the garlic and shallot and chop your herbs.

**3** Now heat the coconut oil and very gently fry the shallot, garlic and tomatoes. Don't let anything brown or burn in the slightest - you're almost just warming it up.

**4** Now that these and the pasta are ready, throw the herbs and leaves into the pan to just slightly get a coating of the oil and flavour and then squeeze over the lemon juice.

**5** Either mix into the pasta or serve on top!

# Tarka Dal

This Indian dish is excellent as a smaller side or as a main.  Packed with protein!

**Serves:** 4
**Preparation Time:** 20 Minutes
**Cooking Time:** 60 minutes

**Ingredients:**
250g yellow dried split peas
1 litre water
3 tbsp coconut oil
1 tbsp cumin seeds
1 small onion
3-4 whole green chillies
2cm fresh ginger
3 garlic cloves
3 tomatoes
¾ tsp ground turmeric
¾ tsp garam masala
1½ tsp ground coriander
Sea salt and ground black pepper
Handful coriander leaves

## Instructions:

**1** Prepare the split peas by rinsing them thoroughly until the water runs clear.  Now cook them by placing in a pan with 900ml of the water and bring to the boil.  As it boils a foam may appear on the top - scoop this off as it does.  Now cover and simmer, stirring occasionally for about 40 minutes.  Add more water if necessary.

**2** While this is happening, prepare all of your vegetables.  Slice the onion, prick holes in the chillies, peel and cut the ginger into thin strips, peel the garlic (but leave it whole) and chop the coriander.

**3** Now that the lentils are cooked, grab a whisk and break them down a little to make a thickish texture.  Don't mash them completely, just break them up a little.    Put this to one side to cool.

**4** Next you need to heat the oil to a medium to low heat and fry the cumin seeds for half a minute before adding the chilli, onion and ginger.  Continue to cook for another four to five minutes.

**5** In a food processer, blend the tomatoes and garlic to make a puree and then add this to the pan alongside the ground spices.  Now add the further 100ml of water and bring to a simmer for five to ten minutes before adding your salt and pepper to taste.

Finally, mix in the split peas and throw on the coriander.

# Hearty Lentil & Butternut Squash Stew

This is warming, filling and hearty.  It is a great winter meal when you need that warmth inside you.

**Serves:** 4
**Preparation Time:** 45 Minutes

**Ingredients:**
225g brown lentils
2 brown onions
750ml wheat-free vegetable stock
4 carrots
1/2 butternut squash
1 sweet potato
2 small white potatoes
1 stick of celery
Handful fresh garden peas
Handful watercress
2 tbsp fresh dill
1 tsp Bragg or tamari sauce

**Instructions:**

**1** Start by soaking the lentils for 20 in cold water.  While they are soaking, prepare the vegetables by chopping the onion finely, chopping the carrot into rings, peeling and deseeding the squash, peeling and dicing the potatoes and chopping the celery.

**2** Now you're ready to start cooking!  Put the onions in a large pan with the stock and get this boiling.

**3** Next add the lentils, potatoes, squash and carrot and once this is boiling turn it down to simmer for about fifteen minutes.  Then add the lovely celery and simmer it for another couple of minutes.

**4** Finally, you can add the sauce (Bragg or Tamari) the fresh peas, leaves and dill.

# Cous Cous with Tomato, Basil & Lentils

**Serves:** 4
**Preparation Time:** 30 Minutes

**Ingredients:**
350ml of fresh vegetable juice
(tomato, cucumber, spinach etc)
350ml of alkaline/filtered water
3 cloves of garlic finely chopped
1 tablespoon of olive/avocado oil
or Udo's Choice
220g of lentils (tinned or prepared
yourself from dried)
3 large tomatoes
A big handful of basil leaves, torn
or chopped
200g of uncooked cous cous
A pinch of Himalayan salt
(or sea salt)
A pinch of freshly ground black
pepper

## Instructions:

**1** This is really easy. Firstly steam fry the garlic in a little water until it is softened, just a minute will do.

**2** Then stir in the veggie juice, lentils, water, salt and pepper. Bring this to a simmer to cook the lentils through. Remove from the heat.

**3** Now you can simply chuck in the lentils, tomatoes and basil - cover it up and let it stand for five mins until the cous cous is cooked through.

**4** Lastly, remove the cover and fluff up the cous cous with a fork and you're ready to go!

Works awesomely as a side or as a main with a large salad.

# Aubergine Pizza

**Serves:** 4
**Preparation Time:** 30 Minutes

**Ingredients:**
1 large aubergine (eggplant)
2 tomatoes
2 cloves garlic
1 red or green pepper
1/2 red onion
Tomato paste/puree
Handful of black olives
Handful of basil
Enough rocket to add a little to each pizza
Coconut oil to cook with and olive oil to dress with
Himalayan/Sea salt & black pepper

**Instructions:**

**1** Firstly, preheat the oven to 180 degrees. Now cut the aubergine into 2/3 cm slices, brush with oil and soften in the oven for about 15-20 mins - keep testing them to make sure they're softening up. If it is taking too long or you're impatient you can do them in a griddle pan - this way only takes 5-10 mins.

**2** Next, you just want to soften the toppings, so put the chopped tomatoes, garlic, pepper, half of the basil and red onion into a small pan with a tiny bit of coconut oil and a tablespoon of water.

**3** Soften these down for just a minute or two. Now place bundles of the ingredients onto the aubergine slices and put back into the oven for about 5 minutes.

**4** Once it is all looking hot and tasty, remove from the oven, top with the rocket and remaining basil, drizzle the olive oil, add a little salt and pepper and enjoy!

# Stuffed Tomatoes (Alkaline Style)

**Serves:** 2
**Preparation Time:** 30 Minutes

**Ingredients:**
2 nice big tomatoes
Half a small aubergine
A large handful of fresh spinach
½ onion
1/3 of a courgette
1-2 cloves garlic
1 tbsp. cold pressed extra virgin olive oil or avocado oil
Pinch of sea salt and pepper (pref Himalayan Salt)

**Instructions:**

**1** Firstly, preheat your oven to 160°C (325°F). Next cut the aubergine and courgette up nice and small into little chunks and roughly chop the onion and garlic.

**2** Mix in a bowl with the spinach which you can either leave whole or tear roughly. Season this and add the oil and get your hands right in there to give it a good mix up.

**3** Next top the tomatoes and scoop out the middle bit. Chuck the middle bit in with your other mix and mix it all around nicely. Now you need to carefully stuff this all back into the tomatoes.

**4** Once you're convinced not another tiny bit could fit into the tomatoes, put them into a large pan with about 80ml of water and cover it with a lid. Put this into your preheated over and cook for 15-20 mins. How easy is that?!

Pretty much everything is alkaline, not overly cooked and when served with a nice big salad makes for a nice healthy, alkaline meal!

# Alkaline Ratatouille

**Serves:** 4
**Preparation Time:** 30 Minutes

**Ingredients:**
3 decent sized aubergines
3 medium courgettes
2 red peppers
5 tomatoes, diced
3 tsp thyme leaves
2 cloves of garlic
2 massive handfuls of baby spinach
A handful of basil leaves
10 coriander seeds
A big handful of pitted black olives
Organic extra virgin olive oil
Himalayan salt & black pepper

## Instructions:

**1** Firstly cut the tops and bottoms off the aubergines and courgettes. Now slice the aubergines and courgettes by standing them on their end and slicing the skin and a little bit (about 2-4mm) of flesh.

**2** This is all you'll use of the vegetable in this meal, so use the flesh for my Baba Ganoush recipe on page 125 and the courgette hummous on page 126! How convenient! So firstly, get the garlic chopped up nice and fine.

**3** Now slice the aubergines and courgettes again (keeping separate) so that they're in little cubes about 3mm x 3mm. Nice little shapes. Now put these to one side.

**4** At this stage you want to get your grill on and preheating. Now cut the tops and bottoms off the peppers and get rid of the seeds and white bits. Give them a good wash and cut them into thick slices so that you can place them skin side up under the grill.

# Alkaline Ratatouille (continued)

**Serves:** 4
**Preparation Time:** 30 Minutes

**Ingredients:**
3 decent sized aubergines
3 medium courgettes
2 red peppers
5 tomatoes, diced
3 tsp thyme leaves
2 cloves of garlic
2 massive handfuls of baby spinach
A handful of basil leaves
10 coriander seeds
A big handful of pitted black olives
Organic extra virgin olive oil
Himalayan salt & black pepper

**Instructions:**

**5**  Once they're blackened, pop them in a bowl and cover with cling film for five mins. After that time you should be able to get the skins off nice and easy. Now dice them up to match the courgettes and aubergines.

**6**  Now you need to get these the aubergine cooking. So heat a little olive or coconut oil in a pan (preferably coconut as this is less effected when heated) and gently cook along with one clove of garlic.

**7**  After cooking the aubergine all at once, put into a sieve and press with kitchen paper towels to get out any excess oil. Now add a little more oil to the pan and do the same with the courgette and the other clove of garlic.

**8**  Now mix in a large pan with the other ingredients and warm very gently. I like to keep the tomatoes raw and throw the spinach in right at the last minute so it just wilts a little.

Serve with a big salad and voilà!

# Alkalizing Catalan Stew

**Serves:** 4
**Preparation Time:** 10 Minutes

**Ingredients:**
6 tbsp olive oil
1 large Spanish onion, chopped
2 fennel bulbs, chopped
1 red chilli, finely chopped
1 tsp fennel seeds, ground
2 cloves of garlic, crushed
½tsp sweet paprika powder
1 tbsp fresh thyme leaves
1 tsp saffron strands (optional)
3 fresh bay leaves
1 tin plum tomatoes
250ml/3½ fl oz veg stock or water
650g/1 lb 7 oz firm white fish
(bream, pollock, cod, monkfish),
filleted or tofu
100g/3½ oz toasted almonds,
ground

**To Serve:**
1 lemon, cut into wedges
Quinoa and spring greens

**Instructions:**

**1** Heat some water in a large pan and steam fry the onions, fennel, chilli, ground fennel seeds and garlic for a few minutes.

**2** Add the paprika, thyme, saffron, bay leaves and tomatoes and cook until reduced to a thickish sauce.

**3** Add the vegetable stock (or water) and bring to a simmer.

**4** Put the fish pieces/tofu into the stew and stir in the almonds.

**5** Heat for a minute or two and serve with seasonal greens, quinoa and wedges of lemon.

# Cous Cous Stuffed Peppers

Easy, filling and mostly raw alkaline cous-cous. This one is a life save!

**Serves:** 2
**Preparation Time:** 15 Minutes

**Ingredients:**

**For Peppers:**
2 red peppers (capsicums)
2 cups of cous cous
1 red onion (small)
2 cloves of garlic
2 tomatoes
A dash of Bragg Liquid Aminos
(or soy sauce)
1 tablespoon of olive oil
Coconut oil
Salt & pepper
Optional: sprinkling of sultanas

**For the salad:**
Handful of baby spinach
Handful of rocket
Handful of watercress
1 avocado
½ cucumber

**For the dressing:**
Juice of 1 lemon
Olive oil to taste
1 clove of garlic, very finely
chopped
Salt & pepper

**Instructions:**

**1** First, wash the peppers and chop them in half, either way. Now lightly rub a very small amount of olive oil over them with your hands and place under the grill to cook until warm and cooked but still quite firm.

**2** Now, chop the onion finely, along with the garlic and slice the tomato into small chunks.

**3** Then prepare the cous cous according to the packet instructions (or boil 2 cups of water, then add cous cous, removing from the heat and let stand for two minutes. Then return to a very low heat, add a tablespoon of olive oil and stir with a fork to separate grains).

**4** While this is preparing gently warm the onion, garlic, tomatoes and optional sultanas in coconut oil in a pan.

**5** Once these ingredients have all softened add the cous cous and turn the heat right down. Add extra olive oil, the Bragg and salt & pepper to taste. Now fill the peppers and serve with the salad and dressing!

# Snacks & Dressings

Snacks are probably the most important thing to have available when you first start alkalising. I have found that the most number of people slip up when transitioning because they do not have good, quick and tasty alkaline snacks on hand when they are hungry between meals and end up reaching for something naughty.

These snacks should keep you going and are all 100% healthy and full of nutrients.

There is no need to fear the snack attack again!

# Alkaline Nachos

I bet you never though you'd be allowed nachos on the alkaline diet!

**Serves:** 2
**Preparation Time:** 20 Minutes

**Ingredients:**
Sprouted wheat tortillas
Avocado/guacamole
Tomatoes
Red chilli pepper/jalapeños
1/2 can kidney beans
1 spring onion

Note: Sprouted wheat tortillas are not available in many parts of the UK. If you cannot find them, use the best, most healthy wraps you can find (i.e. yeast or gluten-free, wholemeal, organic etc)

**Instructions:**

**1** Lightly toast the sprouted wheat tortillas to make crisp and warm.

**2** Mash the avocado and spread over the tortillas.

**3** Next, cover with diced fresh tomatoes, thinly sliced chilli/jalapeños, the drained and washed kidney beans and the thinly sliced spring onion.

Season to taste and enjoy!

# Alkaline Pesto Perfection

Amazing, tasty sauce to use in any meal, salad or side

**Serves:** 2
**Preparation Time:** 15 Minutes

**Ingredients:**
1 cup of pine nuts
2 cloves of garlic
1 large bunch of basil (or more to suit your taste)
Olive oil to suit desired consistency
Himalayan salt and cracked black pepper

**Instructions:**

**1** Wash all ingredients and blend, starting with the basil, pine nuts and garlic. Keep adding oil until desired consistency is reached. Season to taste.

**2** Use to coat veggies, with a small brown pasta side or as a dip.

# Raw Alkaline Tahini

Another versatile dip/sauce that is full of nutrients

**Serves:** 2
**Preparation Time:** 10 Minutes

**Ingredients:**
1 cup of sesame seeds
75ml of alkaline water
4 tbsp flax seed oil
Himalayan salt to taste

**Instructions:**

**1** Grind, blend or mash sesame seeds to form a moist meal and then mix with other ingredients to form a nice, thick paste.

# Dressed to Impress Asparagus

Quick and easy, this snack can be part of a main meal or a sexy-libido-boosting side dish

**Serves:** 2
**Preparation Time:** 10 Minutes

**Ingredients:**
12 asparagus stems
8 spring onions
2 tablespoons melted (avocado)
butter
Grated lemon peel of half a lemon
Fresh lemon juice of 1 lemon
Fresh thyme

**Instructions:**

**1** Lightly steam the asparagus and spring onion together (for about 4 minutes or until as tender as you like - although remember, overcooking removes nutrients!).

**2** Then, mix together the avocado butter, lemon rind, juice and thyme to make a dressing. If it is too zingy, then add some cold-pressed extra virgin oil to neutralize the lemon a little.

**3** Now decoratively stack the asparagus and spring onion and dress.

# Garlic Dressing

A great dressing for salads, veggies or anything you want to give that garlic zing

**Serves:** 2
**Preparation Time:** 10 Minutes

**Ingredients:**
1 clove of garlic
1 lemon
2 tbsp avocado oil
Himalayan salt and black pepper

**Instructions:**

**1**  Crush the garlic clove and in a small bowl thoroughly mix with the juice of lemon, the avocado oil and the seasoning.

**2**  Leave to infuse for 8 minutes before serving over a salad, vegetables etc.

**3**  Feel free to play with the quantities of lemon juice to oil to suit your tastes.

# Veggie Sticks & Hummous

My most frequently enjoyed snack - this is a tasty treat for any occasion!

**Serves:** 2
**Preparation Time:** 10 Minutes

**Ingredients:**

**For the hummous:**
1 can or equivalent weight
of dried chickpeas (soaked
according to instructions)
1 tablespoon of tahini (p112)
1 clove of garlic
Lemon juice from 1/2 a lemon
1 tablespoon of olive oil

**For the sticks:**
1 carrot
1/2 cucumber
1 pepper (red, green or yellow)
1 celery stick

**Instructions:**

**For the hummous:**

**1** Prepare the chickpeas and then blend with the remaining ingredients in a hand blender. Add Himalayan salt and cracked black pepper to taste.

Variation: add fresh tomatoes or chilli just before blending.

**For the sticks:**

**2** Thinly slice all of the vegetables, making sticks thin enough to have plenty of dips with, but thick enough to be able to hold the weight of plenty of dip!

# Hummous from Heaven

Fast, versatile & very tasty

**Serves:** 2
**Preparation Time: 10** Minutes

**Ingredients:**
1 can of chick peas (or home cooked chick peas)
1 tablespoon of Tahini (p112)
Small clove of garlic (crushed or finely chopped)
Lemon juice from 1/2 Lemon (or to taste)
1 tablespoon olive oil

**Instructions:**

**1** Put all ingredients in a bowl and blend with one of those nice fast whizzy hand blenders.

**2** Season with Salt and Pepper to taste

Variations:

Add handful of black olives before blending

or

Change chick peas for butter beans

or

Adding fresh tomatoes before blending

# Mexican Sweet Potato Chips

This really is a treat and is just so tasty - one of my newest recipes that I just adore!

**Serves:** 2
**Preparation Time:** 35 Minutes

**Ingredients:**
1 large sweet potato
1 avocado
1 tomato
1 tbsp sesame seeds
1 tbsp olive oil
Paprika

**Instructions:**

**1** Preheat your oven to 210 degrees.

**2** Thoroughly wash the sweet potato (don't peel) and then slice thinly to make rough chips.

**3** Put the chips into a large dish and lightly coast in olive oil and Himalayan salt. Mix so that every chip has a light coating.

**4** Bake the chips until crisp and golden.

**5** While the chips are baking, finely slice the tomato and red onion and peel the avocado. Mix and mash these ingredients together in a bowl along with the sesame seeds and olive oil.

**6** Once you remove the chips from the oven, top each with the avocado mix or use the mix as a dip and sprinkle with paprika.

# Delicious Omega Dressing

A great, tasty way to get your essential omega 3's!

**Serves:** 2
**Preparation Time:** 30 Minutes

**Ingredients:**
2 tablespoons of Udo's Choice or
flax oil (cold pressed)
1 large (or 2 small) cloves of
garlic, crushed
Juice of 1/2 lemon
Sprinkle of Himalayan salt
Cracked black pepper

Instead of salt and pepper, use
Herbamare - a combination of
organic herbs and sea salt.

**Instructions:**

**1**   Here's a simple, healthy way to liven up a bowl of your favourite fresh pasta.

You can make up a big batch and store, but keep it in an airtight container because the oil will go toxic if exposed to light, air or heat.

Simply mix all ingredients and mash in the garlic.

Enjoy!

# Basil & Coriander Dressing

This slightly spicy, herby delight is great for salads, pastas or just on top of veggies!

**Serves:** 2
**Preparation Time:** 35 Minutes

**Ingredients:**
1 bunch of coriander
1/2 bunch of basil
2 cloves of garlic
1 chilli (or to taste)
Himalayan/Sea salt
Black pepper
Organic extra virgin olive oil

**Instructions:**

**1** This is really easy - just put everything into a blender, except for half of the oil.

**2** Now blend it up! Keep adding more oil to get the consistency you want.

**3** Add the chilli a bit at a time if you're not sure how hot you want it!

# Smooth Almond Pate

This delicious pate is easy to make and wonderfully decadent!

**Serves:** 4
**Preparation Time: 10** Minutes

**Ingredients:**
200g whole almonds, presoaked in water overnight
75g pine nuts
2 tbsp lemon juice
2 tbsp olive oil
1 garlic clove, peeled and crushed
3 tbsp chopped fresh basil

**Instructions:**

**1** Having soaked your almonds overnight, they'll now be nice and plump, so drain them and blend them with all the other ingredients and 2 tablespoons of water until it is all nice and smooth.

**2** Now, place in the fridge in a nice looking bowl until you want to serve! Should keep for 2-3 days. I like to enjoy with sprouted breads and crackers.

# Unreal Minty Dressing

**Serves:** 2
**Preparation Time:** 30 Minutes

**Ingredients:**
10 tablespoons of olive oil (or a mix of olive, avocado and Udo's Choice)
5 tablespoons of fresh lemon (squeezed yourself, not packaged)
1 big handful of finely chopped mint (fresh)
3 teaspoons of tahini (p112)
70ml of water
Salt & pepper to taste

**Instructions:**

**1**    Blend all of the ingredients together until smooth! Done!

# Gluten Free Pumpkin Bread

It is a great one to have in summer or winter with soups, stews or just with avocado and tomato!

**Serves:** 2
**Preparation Time:** 30 Minutes
**Cooking Time:** 2 Hours

**Ingredients:**
1 small pumpkin
300g gluten-free flour
2 tsp baking powder
1 tsp of Italian seasoning
2 tbsp of oil (udo's choice, hemp oil, flax oil etc)
50-75ml of water

**Instructions:**

**1** First and foremost, the oven must be preheated to 200C (or gas mark 6). Once this has preheated, put the entire pumpkin onto a baking tray and bake for at least 40-50 minutes or until the pumpkin has become quite soft.

**2** Cool the pumpkin (still on the tray) for at least half and hour.

**3** Remove the skin from the pumpkin, cut out the stalk and remove the seeds. Mash the pumpkin well, and then stir in the remaining ingredients.

**4** Next, put the pumpkin onto a floured surface and knead until the mixture becomes sponge-like. If it feels too sticky, add a little more water.

**5** Shape the mixture into a circular loaf shape and place on a lightly oiled baking tray. Make a pattern in the top of the loaf such as a cross.

Bake for 30-40 minutes or until done (you can tell by tapping the base of the loaf - if it sounds hollow, it is ready).

# Courgettes in chick-pea sauce

Surprisingly flavourful & delicious snack that is ready in under 15 minutes

**Serves:** 2
**Preparation Time:** 20 Minutes

**Ingredients:**
120g quinoa
2 tablespoons olive oil
400g courgettes, sliced diagonally
1 handful fresh coriander or parsley, ripped
2 tablespoons sesame seeds

**For the sauce:**
400g chick-peas, drained and rinsed
1 large tomato or 3 cherry
1 garlic clove
1 tablespoon lemon juice
Drizzle of olive oil
1 tablespoon of water
½ teaspoon chilli powder
½ teaspoon cumin powder
100g tofu

## Instructions:

**1** Cook the quinoa by adding 1 part quinoa to 2 parts water, bringing to the boil and then simmering and covering for 10 minutes or until all the water is evaporated.

**2** Put all the sauce ingredients in a blender and blitz until smooth, adding a little more olive oil if necessary or a little more water.

**3** Put a small amount of water in a large frying pan and steam fry the courgettes for a few minutes.

**4** Add the sauce and warm through. Add the olive oil in just before serving.

**5** Divide the courgettes between two plates, top with herbs.

**6** Add the quinoa and sprinkle the seeds over the top, drizzle with a little more olive oil and season to taste!

# Alkaline Tomato Salsa

Fresh, funky and great to use on a million meals!  This is a real staple salsa.

**Serves:** 8
**Preparation Time:** 15 Minutes

**Ingredients:**
8 large tomato
3 jalapeño or chilli peppers
3 garlic cloves
1 onion
2 limes, juiced
2 teaspoons Himalayan/sea salt
1 tablespoon ground cumin
1 tablespoon chilli powder
6 sun-dried tomatoes
Small handful of coriander
Small handful of basil
½ a red and yellow pepper
Olive oil

**Instructions:**

**1**  Roughly chop the coriander and basil, tomatoes, onion, and peppers.  Slice the garlic clove and de-seed the chillies.

**2**  Throw everything into a small blender and blend to get the consistency you like.

**3**  Add a little olive oil to alter the texture if you like and serve with any of the meals in this recipe book!

# Sun-Dried Tomato Paste

**Serves:** 4
**Preparation Time:** 15 Minutes

**Ingredients:**
1 cup of soaked sunflower seeds
1/3 cup soaked sun-dried tomatoes
2 tablespoons water
1 tablespoon finely diced red
onion
1 tablespoon freshly squeezed
lemon juice
2 teaspoons chopped fresh basil
1 clove garlic roughly chopped or
smacked flat
1/4 teaspoon Himalayan salt
Sprinkle of black pepper

**Instructions:**

**1** Soak all of the soaked ingredients beforehand (for a few hours
or overnight) and then put into a food blender with the little bit of
water.

**2** Now blitz it into a paste! Transfer all of this to a bowl and stir in
the remaining ingredients! Done!

Enjoy!

# Alkaline Baba Ganoush!

**Serves:** 4
**Preparation Time:** 30 Minutes

**Ingredients:**
1 very large aubergine
1-2 cloves of garlic (dependent on personal preference)
Juice of 2 lemons
2 tablespoons of tahini
A handful of parsley
Himalayan salt & black pepper to taste

**Instructions:**

**1**  Firstly, give the aubergine a good wash, but leave it completely intact. Now give the skin a prick with a sharp knife in a few places and grill it whole for about half an hour. Turn it every five minutes or so.

**2**  After 30 mins the skin should be blackening and you'll know its ready because it should be kind of deflating!

**3**  Once it's done, slice the end off and let it cool a little. Now cut into it and scrape the lovely insides off of the flesh with a spoon and put the flesh into a colander for a few minutes to let it drain out a little.

Now throw everything into a blender together and blend up until smooth! Easy!

# Courgette (Zucchini) Hummous

**Serves:** 4
**Preparation Time:** 30 Minutes

**Ingredients:**
1 tin of chickpeas, drained and
rinsed OR equivalent dried chickpeas soaked and prepared
1 green courgette, chopped
1 garlic clove, chopped
Handful chopped parsley
Handful chopped basil
Himalayan or Sea Salt
Freshly ground black pepper
4 tbsp olive oil
Squeeze of fresh lemon juice

**Instructions:**

**1** Simply put everything in a blender and whizz it up until it looks
how you like your hummous! The addition of basil is genius - so
if you like your basil then add a little more!

# This Is Not The End!

I truly hope that this recipe book has provided you with the inspiration and enthusiasm to make the alkaline diet a permanent part of your lifestyle.

I thoroughly enjoyed creating this collection and these recipes have all played a big part in my diet over the past eleven years.

BUT...as you might have already seen or heard, my site, liveenergized.com is packed full of free guides, resources, videos and teaching, all aimed at helping you nourish your body, and make it easy, enjoyable and achievable to get to the health, vitality and body of your dreams...the health you deserve!

# What's Next?

This is just the beginning!  No matter where you are on your health journey, I strongly recommend you head over to www.liveenergized.com and immerse yourself!

You'll find more delicious recipes, guides, hundreds of video tutorials, plus access to:

- The Alkaline Starter Guide (including 2x workbooks and 3 videos)
- The Definitive Guide to Alkaline Water
- The Complete Acid/Alkaline Food Chart

Plus so much more!  There are literally over a thousand guides, articles and resources for you, all completely for free.  Plus, you can contact me directly and get onto one of my frequent Q&A Coaching Calls (Webinars) and talk to me direct!

Until then, stay alkaline
Ross